I Knew This Place

Radio Essays from Sunday Miscellany

John MacKenna

The Harvest Press

I Knew This Place

By John MacKenna

Published in 2020

by The Harvest Press

www.theharvestpress.ie

Copyright 2020 John MacKenna

ISBN 978-1-8380836-0-1

Illustrations: Katie Jacques

Cover Illustration: Joe Bray

Introduction

Over the past decade, John MacKenna has been a regular and highly popular contributor to the RTE Radio 1 programme *Sunday Miscellany*.

His radio essays, dealing with everything from orchard robbing to the brevity of life; from leather footballs to ghosts inhabiting his car, are peopled with memorable characters, many of them living on the periphery of society. These are the men and women who faithfully stood in the rain to watch *The Late Late Show* on a silent television in a shop window; they are the young boys who ran away to join carnivals and circuses; the girls who sat in a darkened cinema dreaming of better and brighter futures; the man so removed from society that Christmas passed him by.

The essays explore the area around MacKenna's hometown of Castledermot and the people who lived there and then, suddenly, take us to other places and introduce us to other people. We climb the side of a Greek mountain; we meet Leonard Cohen and Lev Yashin. We travel to the moon. The more than eighty essays in this collection – in prose and verse – gather the best of MacKenna's contributions to *Sunday Miscellany* into one compelling collection.

For Oscar, Isabel and Isaac
who will have their own stories to tell.

I knew this place, I knew it well,
Every sound and every smell,
And every time I walked I fell
For the first two years or so.

There across the grassy yard,
I a young boy runnin' hard,
Brown and bruised and battle
Scarred and lost in sweet illusion.

From my window I can see
The fingers of an ancient tree,
Reaching out it calls to me
To climb its surly branches.
But all my climbing days are gone
And these tired legs I'm standin' on
Would scarcely dare to leave the spot upon
Which they are standin'.

And I remember every word
From every voice I ever heard,
Every frog and every bird,
Yes, this is where it starts.
A brother's laugh, the sighing wind,
This is where my life begins,
This is where I learned to use my
Hands and hear my heart.

This house is old, it carries on
Like lyrics to an old time song,
Always changed but never gone
This house can stand the seasons.
Our lives pass on from door to door,
Dust upon the wooden floor,
Feather rain and thunder roar,
We need not know the reason.

And all these thoughts come back to
Me, like ships across a friendly sea,
Like breezes blowing endlessly
Like rivers running deep.
The day is done, the lights are low,
The wheels of life are turning slow,
And, as these visions turn and go,
I lay me down to sleep.

I Knew This Place
David Mallett

Spring

Billy O

Life was less than kind to Billy O. Right from the word go the road ahead curved ever upwards, the incline getting steeper, the inevitable end a sheer cliff face that offered nothing after all. But for that one spring, and the year that followed, the light shone brightly on Billy's golden dreams.

It was an afternoon in April and we were in the school playground when the carnival arrived in Castledermot. The long line of lorries and caravans twisted like a snake-charmer's serpent along the narrow lane to the side of the playground, winding its enticing way towards the Fair Green. We stood goggle-eyed, our games of football and *tig* forgotten, the swinging boats and chair-o-planes bolted securely onto lorries passed us by, offering the promise of the only abandon that would come our way that year or for many years to come.

I can't say I was aware of Billy O that afternoon. He was in seventh-class, the holding pen for those long-trousered boys who had already decided their education was complete; the boys who would, on the morning of their fourteenth birthdays, empty their schoolbags of the unused copybook or two and the pencil and the nibbed pen and adapt them as lunch bags for the farm-labouring or coal-shovelling that lay ahead.

The following weekend the carnival was in full swing – chair-o-planes zipping through the night air; swinging boats rising and falling creakily; bumper-car poles sparking off the overhead grid; blue and red bulbs flashing above the pongo tent; pink candyfloss magically winding itself around the long sticks that were dipped into the swirling metal bin – excitement and colour and another world of anticipation and exhilaration had come to our village for a week.

And then it was gone. All that remained was the flattened grass and the holes where the hefty pegs of the pongo tent had been buried in the earth and the tyre marks of the heavy lorries like reminders not to put our faith in passing, cravat-wearing prophets.

And Billy O was gone as well. The lure of the road; the possibility of excitement; the offer of a job had met with no resistance. He had run away with the carnival. From what we fourth-class boys heard, a postcard had come to his mother and father from a town on the east coast, saying that he would be in touch.

His parents accepted his decision, realising that the opportunities that awaited him on his fourteenth birthday were far short of the shining, gift-wrapped prospects a young boy would hope for. The best they could offer him was an introduction to agricultural labour or a ticket for the boat to England. The carnival, on the other hand, presented a paying job; a bunk in a caravan and the enjoyment of a new town every week.

Rumours circled the playground that spring. Billy O had left the carnival and joined a circus; he was part of a high-wire act; he had travelled to Russia with the show; he was lion-taming in an American city; he was the world's newest ringmaster. This young boy who had sat at the back of the room in seventh class, head down, biding his time till time itself released him from the anger of the headmaster, had suddenly attained heroic status. We, who wouldn't have kicked a football in his direction, were in awe of his courage and his sense of the possibilities beyond our own slim hopes.

Word came that summer, from returning holidaymakers, that Billy had been seen with the carnival in Tramore. He looked well, he looked older than his fourteen years, he was happy, he sent a big hello to everyone.

The following spring, the carnival snaked its way, again, through the village and the moment school was over we stampeded to the fair green.

And, sure enough, there was Billy O, a cigarette dangling from the corner of his mouth, high on the roof of the pongo tent, tightening the ropes. He ignored us. We were kids and he was a working man.

That weekend Billy was the one in charge of the bumper cars, collecting the money, swinging the steering wheels lightly as he leaned over the shoulders of girls who hung on his every word and giggled when he guided their cars out of dead end corners. The same girls hung around him when the carnival lights dimmed and the night drew to a close and there they were again the following night, basking in his striking glow. Girls who wouldn't have given him the time of day had he been working on a farm or in a shop were suddenly enthralled by everything he said and did. And we, young whippersnappers, were no better.

And then the carnival was gone again – only the flattened grass and the hard words that followed Billy's departure remained. He'd got notions about himself; who did he think he was, *showing off like he owned the bloody carnival*?

The following spring the lorries and caravans returned but there was a different young man working the bumper cars. Life was, indeed, to prove less than kind to Billy O, but for that one spring and the year that followed the light had shone brightly on his golden dreams. I hope he found some way of remembering those days of brightness when the darkness fell. I hope he knew that his heroism is well and fondly remembered by a short-trousered boy from fourth class.

Cashes

Oh, the summertime is comin',
And the trees are sweetly bloomin',
And the wild mountain thyme
Grows around the blooming heather.

Liam Clancy was on the radio, singing "Will You Go, Lassie, Go" and something in his voice or in the words or in the slow, heartfelt music that seems to grow from the depths of the earth brought the Cashes to mind and I couldn't fathom why. All I knew was that it was summer again and I was ten years old and the school desks where the Cash children had sat were empty.

Outside, the sun is shining and the lilac tree that bends and curtsies is waltzing its dancing fragrance and I know I won't see the Cashes again until late autumn.

At three o'clock the bell rings and we burst from Mr Begley's room like a broken vase, scattering in all directions. I let the others go ahead and slip down the Laurels, the walkway that leads me past the drunken headstones, down by the back of Copes' shop and onto the Fair Green. And sure enough, the horse-drawn wagon with its bright and singing colours is gone. Only the neat circle of scorched stones and the cropped grass where the horses grazed remain as mementos of the family who lived here through the autumn and winter and into the early months of spring.

I stand a moment and try to imagine what it must be like to wake up one early summer morning and know that the road has suddenly opened before you; that you have closed the heavy door on the shadowed school corridor and the cold pungent toilets and the bitter parade of disciplined desks.

I imagine what it's like to harness the horses and put them between the shafts of the cart and the wagon and amble out of the sleeping village, into the rising sun; travelling all day, stopping only to rest and eat and feed and water those horses; knowing that tonight you'll sleep in another place and you'll be free.

And wandering back home, passing the empty school, I wonder what it's like to sit on the side of a flat cart and listen, above the slow clopping of the horse's feathered feet, to the prison rote of two plus two is four; four plus four is eight; eight plus eight is sixteen; sixteen plus sixteen is thirty-two; how wonderful to hear the tentative-times tables fade as another town gives way to ditches of splashed whitethorn and banks of primroses and tree-shaded campsites where the scent of bluebells rings out above the smell of firewood.

I know that some autumn morning when the leaves stop raining and the crows cluster on the undressed branches, the Cashes will be back on the Green. Their dogs curled beneath the flat cart, and the low canvas tent where the boys sleep will be in the shelter of a bush and slow smoke will be rising from the chimney above the summer painted sides of the wagon.

But that's all a lifetime away, beyond the dazzling days of June and the poppied roadsides of July, beyond the reach of stubbled August and the mushroomed fields of September. Beyond, even, the last glorious fling that will be October.

For now, I can only wander slowly home, kicking a stone along the dusty School Lane and up through Carlow Gate and into Abbeylands.

For now, the Cashes are free and I envy them that freedom and their unlocked roads and their dogs trotting between the wheels of the low cart.

What I don't know is that they will die young – from TB and pneumonia and winter dampness and malnutrition. From the ravages of the very freedom I so envy in them – the young, suntanned boys who sat in the desks beside me; the laughing, beautiful girls with their heads of golden hair. One kind of freedom will lead to another.

Perhaps it was the summer in that song that took me back, a summer that was shadowed by the darker verse beyond.

Oh, the autumn-time is comin',
And the leaves are gently fallin',
Where the wild mountain thyme
Grows around the blooming heather.

Jack the Basketman

Here we are, almost halfway through the decade of remembrance, and I'm doing my own remembering, recalling a man who this time one hundred years ago was halfway through a war that was to change his life for ever.

Jack Fitzgerald was born somewhere in County Limerick and, for whatever reason, joined the British army at the outbreak of the First World War. By the time it ended, four years later, he had seen things no one should see and his body and mind had been damaged beyond recovery by gas and horror.

I have no idea where he went or what he did in the years that followed the war but, by the time I was a boy of eight or nine, he had washed up on the shores of our little community in County Kildare and was living in a hole in the ground off the narrow side lane that linked the Athy and Dublin roads. His home was a trench, burrowed deep into the corner of an empty field. Its roof a sheet of galvanise. His familiarity with the trenches of France and their relative safety had burned itself into his brain.

I remember damp winter Saturday afternoons when I'd see him from the window of our house traipsing up the Low Terrace. He looked like a skeleton in his thin, dirty overcoat, its lapels pinned tight against the wind and rain. I'd shout the news to my mother.

"Jack the Basketman is coming!" By then he was no longer Jack Fitzgerald. His new name derived from the woven basket he carried on his left arm, a basket that held his means of livelihood.

"Get away from the window and stop staring," my mother would say. Through the net curtain I'd watch him go from door to door and, eventually, his knock would sound on ours. My mother would open the door, hand him a sandwich and some change and take the printed prayer and the paper flower he proffered. "Thank you," my mother would say but the Basketman was silent, always silent. As soon as the door was closed the flower and the prayer were consigned to the burning coals of the range. "Charity or not," my mother would say, "there's no sense in taking chances with TB."

And I remember hot summer afternoons when four or five of us youngsters from the Low Terrace would wind our lazy way up to the Turnpike and stand on the ditch at the edge of the field that held Jack the Basketman's trench. Someone had seen him setting off with his basket of flowers and we dared each other to remove the rocks and lift the heavy iron roof off his home in the ground. Someone faced someone on that ditch and challenged them and someone accused someone of cowardice and, in the end, we contented ourselves with throwing stones against the galvanised sheet, half-expecting the noise to bring the absent Jack shuffling after us.

And, later that summer, I overheard my father talking to a local guard and Jack's name came up in conversation.

"Sometimes he stays in there for days on end," the guard said quietly. "It must be a killer lying there in this heat, in the darkness, afraid to come out, imagining the bullets and the shells bursting all around him."

And now, halfway through this decade of remembrance, I think about that old man – Jack Fitzgerald, Jack the Basketman – and I think of us young boys thoughtlessly flinging stones against the metal roof of the place he called home, cowering in the darkness and the rancid heat; a man so far from his birthplace and so far from reality and I imagine the ghosts who crowded in there with him, the spectres of his comrades who fell in Belgium, at Ypres and Mons. And all I can do, at this remove, is hope that somehow or other he found peace in the quietness of the night and that his mind took him, in those silent hours, to earlier, more tranquil places and happier times, hours spent on the banks of the Maigue or the Shannon, hours when the scream of shells or the thoughtlessness of young boys had not yet scarred his waking life.

My Grandmother's House

I was sorting some CDs in the past week when I came across Judy Collins' album *True Stories and Other Dreams* with its superb song "Secret Gardens of the Heart" and those wonderfully evocative opening lines: *My grandmother's house is still standing, though it isn't the same.*

Every time I hear those lines they take me back to my own grandmother's house in Church View in Tuam, that solid, early twentieth century dwelling, built for my train-driving grandfather, Tim, and his wife, Brigid McHugh, when they moved from Sligo to the smoky Galway town. And the things I remember most are the details of the yard outside the back door, an enclosed area that led through a rose-scented arch to the fertile, rambling garden which backed onto the cattle mart. Beyond the mart, the spire of the Church of Ireland rose into the sky and gave the house and the road on which it was built a name.

In the yard was the low turf shed that smelled of summer all year round, the warm, peaty scent trapped between the timber walls and the genuflecting roof. Its floor was soft beneath the feet, fifty years of turf mould had tempered the earth, making it pliable and welcoming each time I stepped into the musky twilight to fill the turf basket for the range that heated the large kitchen and cooked the food we were about to eat.

Outside the door of the shed was a bottomless wooden barrel, in which – or so my grandmother told me – kittens were regularly drowned. Only in my teenage years did I realise that there were no cats about the place and that the warning was simply a ploy to keep small children away from the imagined danger of drowning in the soft rain-water gathered for hair-washing.

11

But the thing I remember most vividly is the headless statue of Blessed Martin de Porres – he hadn't yet attained sainthood – that lurked in the sitting room window, his head resting beside him on the sill.

"Why does Granny keep that statue when it's broken," I'd ask my mother, but the answer never came. Instead, I'd be told to run and play and warned never to ask that question of the woman herself. Not that I'd dare. Brigid McHugh was a small woman but she was feisty. Sharp was a word that well described her. She was always welcoming and often kind but Church View was her ship and she ran it by her rules. Once, when my older brother, Jarlath, a third-year student at the time, missed the 11 pm curfew, the doors were locked and that was that, as far as Granny Bray was concerned. If you're not in, you can't sleep beneath the Church View roof.

So, in the long summer days, I played in the shadow of the headless Martin, catching his eye from time to time, wondering why someone hadn't tried to fix him, tempted to glue his head on backwards, just to see if anyone would notice but knowing I never would.

Years later, I think around the time my grandmother died, I heard, at last, the full story of the statue.

One of my aunts had been taken seriously ill in the early nineteen sixties and my grandmother had prayed for a cure to Martin de Porres, a man to whom she had a huge devotion and a man in whom she had total faith. But the cure never came and her daughter, still a young woman with a very young family, died.

When the news came, my grandmother flung the statue against the sitting-room wall in a fit of anger and desolation, smashing the head from the body. Later, regretting the fact that she had blamed the hapless (and headless) Martin for her daughter's death, she put him on the back window of the sitting-room, his head beside him but facing away from her, so that

12

whenever she entered the room she wouldn't meet his gaze – a kind of compromise of exclusion that didn't cast him into external darkness but left him with a lot to think about, even if his head was now beside his ankle.

Even when Martin was canonised in 1962, the promotion went unrecognised in Church View and he sat, still headless, still facing away from those who very occasionally entered the best room.

Now and then, when I'm west of the Shannon, I take a trip to Tuam and I always stop and walk the perimeter of the garden, much changed now. And, of course, I think of my grandmother and I think of summer days in the yard, watched over by the statue of Blessed Martin de Porres. And, I imagine my grandmother sighing a deep, sad sigh for the loss of her youngest child.

Crows

The wake of crows is there above me day on day,
in the high branches of morning,
sycamore and chestnut while they stand –
the same sad keeners who have creaked and carped
for centuries
without ever being tempted into song.
The weight of a world is on their wings,
their argument a great depression in the sky,
the irritable eyes, astute, stare down
or out
across the river to the mountains.
But this is where they live,
their nests a thickening in the arteries of trees,
their bitter conversations most raucous at this hour,
the short, sharp flights begin and end in clamour.

When the lingering dance of night commences,
they will fall into a silence that is nothing more
than the hushed rehearsal of tomorrow's sad complaint.

Back in the Garden

It was three weeks before Christmas and we were wandering out of the Arboretum Garden Centre in Leighlinbridge, having enjoyed a cup of coffee and a scone. I was relaxed, safe in the knowledge that winter is deep and we were in the absolute depths of that quiet time. And then it happened. My constant companion spotted some photographs on the notice-board, photographs of prize-winning gardens.

"That's it," she said, dragging me towards the board, pointing to a photograph of a deep, rich border of wonderful flowers, sweeping like a psychedelic sickle around the edge of a lawn and away towards a beautifully thatched cottage. "That's the kind of border I was trying to explain to you – for our back garden."

"But there's the thatched cottage and the trees and a much bigger lawn," I said, flailing for some excuse. "That's the real attraction."

"I know, I know, but done to scale in our garden it would be beautiful."

By that evening there were eight A4 sheets with designs on the kitchen table and a dozen bamboo rods laid out in various shapes around the garden, to show me what needed to go where. But still, I thought, there's safety in the dark days and I mentioned a horticulturalist acquaintance who always advises against being too early in the garden. "You'll do more harm than good," he says. "You'll compact the soil and set the work back in the long run."

But this week I stepped outside the door and the blackbirds were electric in the hedges and the daffodils – fair daffodils whom we'll weep to see hasten away too soon once my supervised reconstruction work starts – are well above ground, the odd one already threatening to burst into bloom and the raised beds with their winter cabbages had that forlorn look that says: "Dig me, for God's sake dig me!"

Back in December I'd promised I'd get around to the work in the long run. Where, I always wonder, is the long run? Is it this side or the other of the grave? And, just in case it's the latter rather than the former, I find myself unable to resist the call to be outside in the uncertain days of February. And, of course, I may do more harm than good but not to the soil because, by my reckoning, the reconstruction will demand at least a hundred barrows of clay. I know what lies ahead – having already constructed the self-same garden just three years ago! The first few evenings will be a dance with the devil in my lower back.

But more than any of this, there's the call of the clay, a plea that cannot be resisted, it has a way of coaxing me, a voice that says: *Come on, feel the warmth that's been dormant all winter, find the dryness just below the surface, remember the sensation and everything it promises.*

There's that something in the soil that calls me back. A kind of folk memory that warns me year on year that getting too far from the garden is a dangerous step, one that runs the risk of taking any of us away from the earth with all its powers of recall and all the comfort of its touch.

But it's not just about philosophy and being earthed – it's about the joy of being back in the garden – even the reconstructed garden – making something new of this small plot, planning what each raised bed might produce and when. There's the digging and clearing and then there's the pleasure of standing at the kitchen door, just before darkness, and seeing a plot that was filled this morning with trailing, woody Brussels sprouts turned to fresh, gleaming earth that catches the last rays of the uncertain sun and the attention of the inquisitive robin.

Last year, and against my natural inclination, I was gently pushed towards the idea of a potager – that idea that comes, apparently, from the French baroque period – a garden that mixes flowers and herbs with the vegetables, giving colour and variety where once there was simply the useful and the useable.

I have to confess, I took a good deal of persuading to move from the tried and tested to the variety of this French upstart. But what a difference it made! The rampant colours of the flowers, side by side with the vegetables gave the garden a totally new look.

But, of course, it's not what grows and doesn't grow that's the attraction in these early weeks of spring. It's the soil itself and all its possibility. In a week of back-breaking days, I can watch the winter's wilderness transformed into a shining promise. The garden becomes a book of revelation in itself, the fork driving deep and lifting the clodded earth, breaking it into something fresh and beautiful.

In the long run, who could wish to be anywhere else but deep in the element from which we sprang, the place to which we will return, the thing from which we draw our lives and living – the clay with all its secrets and its hope.

The Castle Cinema

I was taking a group of American students on a walking tour of Castledermot during the summer, traipsing the roads and paths I've trodden ten thousand times in my life, starting the excursion in the grounds of St James' church, moving along through the Laurels, turning left onto Abbey Street, down past the old Vocation School – where I began my teaching career – heading towards the ruins of the Franciscan Friary, the Abbey as it's known locally.

On this particular afternoon, the sun was shining more brightly than I'd seen it shine in a long, long time, throwing its light with abandon through the open door of a rectangular building that houses a car salesroom. I had never seen such light in this former den of darkness and electric imagery and I stopped in my tracks, much to the bewilderment of the two dozen students who were following in my wake. They looked left, wondering what was supposed to be of interest.

"When I was a child," I said, "this was our local cinema – the Castle Cinema."

There were a few mutterings of *Right* and *Cool* from behind me but nothing particularly enthusiastic and I knew what the students were seeing was not what I was seeing. Their attention was already wandering from this building, so like a hundred other car salesrooms they'd seen in the States and in Ireland. But what I was seeing was the past.

Nostalgia is a strange lady, with new ways of painting old things and a habit of hiding in the most unexpected of places. There she was, in the angle of sunlight on the concrete floor and there she was standing again in the remembered hallway inside the door. City cinemas might have *foyers*;

we had a *hall*. And, suddenly, there I was standing in the half-light that took me from the reality of the grey long ago days outside into the magical promise of the darkness within; it took me from the streets of a lost village to the possibility and colour of the Arizona desert.

And what I was hearing was the plink plonk of the old piano, stored in the passageway behind the screen, that passageway that led to the men's toilet. The piano that was never locked and so was hammered again and again as we made our way to and from the toilet. And I was hearing the voice of Frank McDonald, local butcher and gentle cinema bouncer and star, year after year, of the local productions of Gilbert and Sullivan operettas. I was hearing his strong, warm voice telling us he was a pirate king, telling it with such conviction that the following day, when I was sent to his shop for five lean chops and a bone for the dog, I checked twice that he didn't have a sword beneath the block on which he was cutting the meat.

And I was hearing the disco music of the seventies when two local men, Richard Kinsella and Michael Clowry, who now would be labelled entrepreneurs for their sins, reopened the empty building as Trudeau's Discotheque – an *homage* to the then Prime Minister of Canada. I was seeing two twenty-year-old students, Pat Clowry and myself, spinning records as a warm-up act before the band took the stage. And I was seeing the throngs of young people dancing, laughing and kissing, the world was theirs, the night was alive with excitement and possibility and I thought of how many are now lying within the boundaries of the low walls of Coltstown cemetery, a stone's throw out the road.

And then my mind slipped back to the days before Pierre Trudeau, back to the days of the Castle Cinema and Peter Murphy who showed films on Sunday afternoons and nights and again on Wednesdays and Fridays. And I heard the loud voice of the man who went to the matinees and then went, again, to the same film on Sunday nights so that he could call out the last plot twist just before the film reached its climax; and I saw the faces of the scattered souls who were there on Christmas nights – men and women who were derided by many for going to such a place on such a sacred night, and I thought of the lonely rooms those lost hearts had left, and I was glad for them.

And I sat in the sixpenny woodeners and I chanced my remembering arm by dashing back to the luxury of the half-crown seats in the moments between the lights going down and the screen lighting up. And I heard Maureen Kinsella laugh uproariously as Groucho Marx stared us in the eyes. And all the ghostly voices and all the fading images came alive again in that brief and strangely coloured moment before the movie of my memories was flittered into nothingness.

"Are we done here?" a voice asked.

"We are," I said. "We are. For now."

The Trimmings

I grew up in a house where saying the rosary was a daily event. Last thing at night, we'd kneel at the kitchen chairs and my mother would launch into the Joyful or Sorrowful or Glorious mysteries and we, each in turn, would *give out* a decade – the Our Father; ten Hail Marys; and the Glory Be to the Father.

There was no escape. If one of us happened to be heading out early – to a dance or to visit friends or to a film – our mother would always ask: *What time do you expect to be back?* And if the answer was vague – and it often was – the inevitable would follow: *Sure, we'll say the rosary before you go so.* Raised eyebrows or low sighs would be met with a: *You'll be glad of it on your death bed* or, if the outing was of a romantic nature, with: *It might well be the protection you need for a pure and peaceful death!* It was as if she imagined every girl we dated was a potential Lizzie Borden or Lady Godiva.

I remember one such summer evening when we were on our knees in the kitchen. It was about half-past six, and the doorbell rang. One of us was dispatched to answer it and the word came back that a group of election canvassers was outside. *Oh bring them in*, my mother said, *I have a crow to pluck with them.* And so the group of three was ushered into the already crowded kitchen. *We're on the third glorious mystery*, my mother told them. *It'll do ye no harm to kneel down.* Two of the men knelt with us, joining in the responses. The third – the prospective TD and a member of the Church of Ireland to boot – sat silently and respectfully in the corner, his cap on his knee, head bowed, listening in wonder.

And then there was my aunt's dog, Sniper, who, on his regular visits to our house, found the saying of the rosary an appropriate time to test his amorous skills on the legs of those kneeling in prayer – much to our amusement, my aunt's embarrassment and my mother's annoyance. Inevitably, by the second mystery, he'd be banished to the outer darkness of the back kitchen.

The trick for us, of course, was to kneel at a chair that had an old newspaper or a magazine beneath the cushion. It was amazing how interesting stale news became by the third or fourth decade. Any attempt at short-changing the Lord by saying only eight or nine Hail Marys, however, was met with a sharp reminder of how the souls in Purgatory were depending on us for release and, furthermore, if our cutting of corners was the extent of our commitment, we might well expect a long and slow roasting when our own time came.

Nor was the rosary confined to the house – on the short car journey to Athy or Carlow to do the shopping, we'd escape with one decade for a safe journey but the thrice-yearly trips to Tuam brought the full five decades on the outward and return journeys.

But, to be honest, the rosary was the easy part of those nightly prayers. It was the trimmings that tested our endurance – the prayers for all kinds of intentions that were added after the formality of the rosary had ended. I have no definite idea as to when the trimmings began in our house but it was long before my time. I know this because I developed my own system of carbon-dating by checking the years of the deaths of some of the people who were still included in our litanies by the time I'd hit my teens. Anyone in the extended family who had died; any friend or any neighbour was added to our nightly list of the dead and, once added, they could sleep peacefully in the knowledge that they would never be dropped. Being included in my mother's trimmings was like being offered permanent membership of the UN Security Council.

And it wasn't just the dead who were prayed for. Exam intentions for all and sundry; job applications; speedy recoveries and peaceful deaths; the finding of houses or digs; appeals to the Sacred Heart; the Blessed Virgin; St Anthony; St Jude; St Joseph of Cupertino and a rake of other saints about whose seed, breed and generation I'm less certain were seasonal if not nightly inclusions. Now and again a *special intention* would be mentioned but we were never given the details. Special intentions covered everything from out of marriage pregnancies in the village to problems in neighbours' or relatives' relationships.

The special intentions may have come and gone but, up to the day my mother died in 1977, we were still praying nightly for the conversion of Russia.

I look back now at the trimmings and I see them in a different light. In my teens, they were a ten- or twelve- or fifteen-minute nuisance when all I wanted to do was be away out with my friends. But now I see them for what they were: an archive of family and community and, in the case of the conversion of Russia, world events that impinged in some way, great or small, on our village, the school in which my mother taught and the little family unit in which we lived, sometimes in fear of illness, sometimes in anticipation of reward for work done or prayers said but always in the hope that our devotions would be heard, our problems solved and our journey to heaven shortened or, at worst, our time in purgatory curtailed.

John MacKenna

What One Man Can Do

I had the pleasure recently of reading from my work at Limerick City Gallery of Art. It was the first time I'd been in the building since 1970, the year when I sat my Leaving Cert in St Clement's College, a stone's throw up the road.

Back then, free Saturday afternoons were spent in the People's Park, hanging out with friends, or mooching around Savin's record shop, ostensibly in search of something new but, in fact, listening to whatever song happened to be playing in the store. Impoverished musical beggars could ill afford to be choosers.

In 1956, my brother had been sent from our home in County Kildare to St Clement's, carrying not so much his own as our mother's vocation to the priesthood. However, he failed to take to the collar and went on to study medicine instead. In 1965, I was sent as his replacement, again carrying our mother's priestly aspirations. Disappointment number two was to follow for her but my five years in Limerick were to be a wonderful and life-changing experience for me.

Our English teacher at St Clement's was a Galway man, Ray Kearns, and he was inspirational beyond belief. His approach to teaching English was to submerge us in the works we were studying but, more importantly, to encourage us to immerse ourselves in everything and anything literary, theatrical and musical. My memory is that we covered the Leaving Cert course in a gallop between February and June 1970 but in the years and months before that everything was open to us and he sent us in search of ideas and opportunities and possibilities that might, otherwise, never have crossed our minds. As far back as 1968 he staged a production of *The*

24

Merchant of Venice and I was cast in a role I loved – that of Shylock. Gilbert and Sullivan operettas were an annual event and even those, like myself, with only a tenuous grasp of how to stay in tune, found themselves onstage in the roles of pirates, geisha girls and courtiers.

But Ray wasn't just about the tried and trusted. I remember him loaning me the works of T. S. Eliot and Patrick Kavanagh; of Steinbeck and Hemingway; of Sylvia Plath – writers who weren't allowed within an ass's roar of the Inter and Leaving Cert courses of the time.

It was he who encouraged my first, thirteen-year-old theatrical writing venture in 1966 – a short and awful play called *I See His Blood* – and again in 1970 – another short play called *Old Friends*. It was he who gave the gift of confidence, who spurred all of his students to write. On Friday evenings he'd post a list of possible essays on the blackboard but then, to my delight, he'd add: "Or anything you feel strongly about writing yourselves."

It was Ray Kearns who suggested I send my first poems to the *Young Citizen* magazine; it was he who encouraged me to send my angry and political pieces of prose and verse to all kinds of publications, including RTE radio; it was he who cobbled together an unlikely debating team in the throes of our Leaving Cert year, a team that went on to win an All-Ireland title; it was he who got us off study to see works as disparate as *Twelve Angry Men*, *Carousel* and *La Bohéme* onstage in Limerick. It was he, more than anyone, who set me on the road to writing. His encouragement, his passion, his belief instilled in me the possibilities that might never have otherwise been there. His conviction that education was not just about what was "on the course"; his recognition that all literature; all music; all theatre has value was instrumental in instilling in his students a willingness to go out there and try things. Most of all, his philosophy that sometimes we fail in trying but always we learn something from the effort we make has stayed with me in the fifty-three years since our paths first crossed.

And so, when I stood at the podium in Limerick City Art Gallery, preparing to read, many of these memories were running through my head. And then the door opened and I saw the smiling face of Ray Kearns. His arrival made that reading even more special, different and exceptional for me. I was back where it had all begun and I felt a sense of privilege to be reading to and for the one man who had done more than any other to set me on the road to writing. That reading was, for me and from me, a salute of gratitude and appreciation.

Dusters

A couple of weeks ago I had an e mail from a friend, a man I'd been in school with more than fifty years ago.

In the course of that letter he referred to an occasion – one I'd forgotten – when he was humiliated by a teacher. The man had slapped him across the back with his walking stick as he knelt at the blackboard writing lines. It wasn't the pain of the stick on his back that he remembered but the greater pain of his awareness of dust rising from the second-hand jacket his parents had bought for him for school. He wrote of how he remembered the dust motes rising in the sunny air of the classroom and of the deep sense of shame that filled his head and his heart.

In the same week I took my car, with its almost 600,000 kilometres on the clock, to Behan's garage in Castledermot for an overhaul. While Mick was working on the engine, a woman approached me and spoke those dreaded words: "You don't know me, do you?"

In the almost forty years since I finished my brief career as a secondary teacher in the Technical School in Castledermot, I've faced that question with regularity and the passage of time has made it ever more frightening. The names and features of the fresh-faced young men and women I taught have, over the years, transmuted, like my own, into the faces of different people. Older, of course, and lived in, the experiences of the years showing. Faces tanned by sun and washed by rain, lined by worry and then made young again by falling snow.

I looked the woman in the eyes and where, a decade ago, I might have gone in circles before stammering an effort at some name I said, politely: "I'm sorry, I don't."

She offered her name and suddenly the years stepped back and I recognised the face, the voice, the smile.

We chatted for a while, filling in the ledger of lives and deaths, and then she said: "You know, the thing I remember most about your English classes was that you had a really accurate shot with a duster when people were daydreaming. You could land it in a cloud of chalk dust on any desk in the room and I don't believe you ever hit anyone."

"Let's be grateful for small mercies," I said.

Later, driving home, the old engine of the car humming quietly – well-oiled and well attended – I thought of my friend's e mail and I thought about the woman's words in the garage and about the few hundred students who had passed through my prefab room between 1974 and 1980.

I thought of the theatre group we created; of the trips to Stratford-on-Avon; buses to the Abbey Theatre; May Eve hunts for the little people; Gary Wall singing Fernando, unaccompanied, at one of our concerts – one of the bravest young men I have ever met; Noel Lambe playing The Traveller in a short Super-eight film we made of Clifford T Ward's song of the same name; John Costigan bringing a class to a laughing halt with some quick reply to a question of mine; Anne O Neill singing *Lost in France* and making us believe for those few minutes that she truly was.

I thought of the plays we staged; the basketball leagues; the chats when Byron's poems led us through the pathless woods which were much more interesting than anything on the syllabus; of the way I hadn't told any of the students I was leaving and, instead, just slipped away one summer into another career, a silence I later regretted.

But my mind kept returning to my friend's e mail and the woman's memory of the accuracy of my duster throwing and I hoped with all my heart – and *still* hope with all my heart – that I never humiliated anyone who sat in that prefab with its poster-covered walls of Dylan Thomas' poems and student verses. Most of all, I hope that, when the dust of recollection settles, the memories of those former students are good ones ... and that they'll forgive my not always recognising them!

The Magic of the B-Side

There may be some of you who won't have a clue what I'm talking about when I mention the B-Side, so let me explain. Once upon a time, in the darkest recesses of the 1960s and '70s there were circular pieces of vinyl called singles. They were records and on each side of the vinyl disc was pressed a song. The major song, the one the record company hoped would be a hit, was called the A side and the other – often written by the singer him – or herself – was called the B-side.

The first single I ever bought was Scott McKenzie's *San Francisco*. It was released in the early summer of 1967. I had heard it first, surreptitiously beneath the blankets in boarding school, the music weaving in and out between the static of Radio Luxembourg which came and went sporadically on my little transistor radio. And, once I heard the song – written by John Philips of the Mamas and the Papas – I couldn't wait to get my hands on it. The following Saturday, on the pretence of needing a haircut, I made good my escape and bought the single.

Back in school, it was rarely off the communal record player and, as a result, it was a week or two after I'd arrived home for the summer holidays before I got to hear the B-side, a song called *What's the Difference Chapter 1* and I was enthralled and excited. It had never entered my fourteen-year-old head that McKenzie might be anything more than the tuneful mouthpiece of songwriters, but here he was preaching a gospel of freedom and adventure, singing a song he'd written himself about picking up a toothbrush, sneaking down the stairs and hitting the road.

In my teenage mind this was the answer to every family squabble I'd ever had. The open road beckoned and I learned the words fast and sang them as I cycled to and from my summer job as a gardener's assistant at the Cistercian Abbey in Moone, a few miles out the road. That was to be the extent of my break for freedom; Bolton Abbey was to be my San Francisco; the monks my hippy comrades.

But, more than that, the song set me off on many years of finding B Sides that were much more appealing and intriguing than the A sides, songs that are still with me, among them *Maggie May* which was the B-side of Rod Stewart's cover of Tim Hardin's *Reason to Believe* and, later his own wonderful *Mandolin Wind*; *God Only Knows* by the Beach Boys; the Righteous Brothers *Unchained Melody*; Elvis' *Always on my Mind* and *Wooden Heart*; *Not Fade Away* by Buddy Holly; Neil Diamond's extraordinary beautiful *Done too Soon*; Paul Simon's *Flowers Never Bend with the Rainfall* and *For Emily Whenever I May Find Her*; Blood, Sweat and Tears' *Sometimes in Winter*; *Wherever I Lay my Hat* by Marvin Gaye....the list goes on ...or rather it did go on until the single became a thing of the past.

Those days of turning the record over, reading the name of the song and the writer, dropping the needle in the groove and hoping for the best became part and parcel of buying a single in my teens and twenties.

Scott McKenzie went on to write further versions of *What's the Difference*, labelling them *Chapter 2* and *Chapter 3* but, for me, it all began with CBS single number 2816 and that song I found on the B side about finding freedom on the open road.

Song for a Pilgrim

(i.m. Tom Hunt)

The last time we saw you was here at this table,
you were spinning us yarns of the journeys you'd made.
Your big hands were open, the lines mapped your palms
and you spoke of the voyage about to begin.

The Pyrenees rose like a dream in your words,
your heart was out there on the sunlit Sierra
and as I listened I imagined you walking,
your wild, silver beard in the fresh morning breeze.

Your step was contented, your mind always racing,
your memory still on the years put behind.
You were the traveller, your weighty bag flying,
your eyes taking in all there was to be seen.

The last time we spoke, you were laughing, as ever,
refusing to bow to the weight on your soul;
you said we'd talk in the days that would follow,
and you wished me the best as I hung up the phone.

Now you've gone on your journey and this time alone,
I catch a brief glimpse of you rounding a bend
and I hope, when I reach it, I'll find you there, seated,
that smile in your eyes and your hand reaching out.

Two Good Men

I grew up in a time and place that was black and white or occasionally grey. Money was tight. Possibilities were few. Opportunities were scarce and life, as our neighbours across the border in Laois would say, was as flat as a cat's arse in the moonlight.

But into this grey world – or out of this grey world to be more precise – came two men who brought colour, vitality and a new energy to the village, two men who had differing but equally exciting views on the ways in which life could be better, happier and more hopeful and a damn sight brighter.

The first was Peter Murphy, the owner of the Castle Cinema in Castledermot. Peter had spent some time in America and had come back with lots of new ideas. He lived in Dublin and worked for a company there but he also built a house in Castledermot – which, to the astonishment of local people, he named "The White House." And three times a week – on Wednesdays, Fridays and Sundays – he drove from Dublin with films for the cinema, films that brought new names, new places and previously unimagined colour to our lives. Almost as impressive as the films was the fact that he made that seemingly monumental hundred-mile round journey at a time when Dublin was a dim and distant imagination to most of us. But he also brought a personality that was larger than life. His introductions to films; his violin performances between the little and big pictures; his way of running a tight ship which kept us noisy kids in check and his throwaway remarks – "This movie stars Audie Murphy, no relation, and it's one must see" – kept us in awe and, more importantly, gave us hope that one day the colour would seep from the cinema screen and run under the cinema door and into our murky lives.

The second man who brought the prospect of joy was Mick Byrne. Mick was the local insurance man, but that was just by day – after six o'clock he was a driving force in the village. He was the man who founded and led the pipe band, with its two mascots, the Irish Wolfhounds Diseart and Diarmada – wolfhounds in a village where the purest dogs we saw were collies crossed with something unidentifiable. Mick was the man who organised the annual Go-cart championships in Castledermot on Bank Holiday Mondays – the tiny vehicles whizzing dizzily around the course that circled the Fair Green and Hamilton Road and Mahon's Lane, the small engines racing in our ears, the helmeted figures like gladiators as they climbed out of the tiny karts – we had never seen, never even imagined anything like this. And there we were on the tv news! It was Mick Byrne who ran the carnivals on the Green, bringing light and adventure and strange faces and foreign accents to skate across the flatness of our own midland inflections. It was Mick who organised the summer marquee that drew bands we'd only dreamed of seeing and hearing – bands whose records were played on the radio.

Mick Byrne and Peter Murphy were two men, who in their differing ways, gave us reasons to be hopeful. One had gone away and come back with new ideas and one had never left but believed in the possibility that life had more to offer than the thump of a missioner's fist on the edge of a pulpit.

It was Peter Murphy who broke the ban on dancing in Lent. It was Mick Byrne who didn't baulk at the financial and spiritual danger of having the Dubliners sing "Seven Drunken Nights" in the marquee tent while we teenagers, too young to be admitted, loitered in the shadows, waiting to hear the banned verses at last.

Neither man will be much remembered beyond the fallen walls of our village or beyond the scattered boundaries of our parish but within those hedged fields, between those tumbled stones, there is a generation of women and men – myself among them – who remember them, not just with fondness, but with pride in their courage and in gratitude for the doors they opened and the lights they lit: the burning bulb of the film projector that illuminated the world outside and the quieter, dancing bulbs that lit the Fair Green around the marquee, throwing up shadows and shapes that might have been the boundaries of our experience but became the gates to our fulfilment.

I salute their passing ghosts.

Photographer

The photographs I love the most are these,

the fading faces of all lovely ghosts

who came alive to music.

Here they dance again

smiles trapped within the glad confusion of a time stood still.

And here they are in gardens overgrown now,

bright flowers gone to seed,

old apples fallen or grown small with time and setting suns.

The camera shutter closes in another age:

the formal faces scowl or smile or are perplexed

or someone shifts and slips forever into rushed uncertainty.

But the face behind the camera, the eyes that peered and framed,

the hands that froze that moment for a century remain unseen.

Who recorded this or this or this?

Who framed the picture of that family against

the deep of rhododendron?

Who chose the moment to say *Smile*?

Some man, some woman whom we never see,

some blessed figure crouched behind the camera

who stilled these forms and faces for a century,

who made but always stood outside the history.

An Altar Boy at Easter

As an altar boy, I spent a lot of my time in the local church. Early mornings, summer evenings, Sundays for Mass, Wednesdays for devotions; first Fridays and sodality nights; benedictions and first holy communions, confirmations and churchings; matchings, hatchings and dispatchings.

But Easter was always the biggest occasion, with ceremonies on Holy Thursday, Good Friday, Holy Saturday and Easter Sunday, four days of rehearsal and four major performances in the drama that could never be matched.

The statues draped in their purple robes reminded us that Saturday night would be the highlight – the paschal fire; the careful uncovering of the statues. Disaster constantly loomed for us altar boys in the possibility of toppling the Sacred Heart or the Blessed Virgin while attempting to remove the Lenten covers.

But before that, there was the Mass of the Last Supper and drama of the Passion reading on Good Friday.

And that year everything went well, until the afternoon of Holy Saturday.

We gathered, as we always did, at two o'clock, for a full dress rehearsal. Surplices and soutanes carefully ironed; black altar slippers neatly tied; hands and faces washed; hair combed. Everything just right. The curate was not a man to suffer the foolishness of being unprepared.

On the way to the church, I'd seen a frog in the grass at Carlow Gate, picked it up and lodged it in my trouser pocket. When you're eleven years of age you know, instinctively, that a frog will somehow come in handy.

In the church we got dressed and then progressed in pairs up the aisle;

rehearsed the responses; listened to the instructions and then did it all again. And again.

Then there was a lull, while the curate went to sign a Mass card. Sitting on the altar steps, I quietly eased the frog from my pocket and slid it gently between the shirt and skin of the boy beside me. For a few seconds nothing happened and then a scream echoed to the rafters of the church and the boy went dancing across the altar, doing a reasonable imitation of Chubby Checker, struggling to free himself of the cold slime against his skin. Surplice and soutane came off; jumper and shirt were torn from his back and the frog hopped onto the altar carpet. Everyone laughed.

Everyone that is except the curate. The noise had brought him running from the vestry.

"What is going on?" his voice boomed.

"There was something down my back, Father," the shirtless boy stammered.

The curate spotted the frog, eyeing him from the altar step.

"And who precisely is responsible for this?"

Silence.

"I am, Father." I knew I was in big trouble. "It was a joke."

"In God's house, on God's altar, on this day of all days. Take that creature and release it and then hang your surplice and soutane in their place. And then go home. You are suspended from altar duties…indefinitely."

"Ah, Father, please, please…."

"Go. Now."

I trudged home, talking to the frog, before releasing it at Carlow Gate, where I'd found it an hour before. And then I faced the music and told my parents what had happened, expecting the worst.

"Me ould segocia," my father laughed, putting his arm around me. "It's time that man took himself a bit less seriously. If that's the worst that ever happens, he'll be doing well. And, anyway, won't you be able to watch the whole shebang from the gallery on Saturday night."

I didn't tell him, couldn't tell him, that the gallery wasn't the place to be, that the only place from which to be involved in the wonderful drama and theatre of the Easter ceremonies was outside the door as the Paschal fire blazed; in the centre aisle while the procession moved through the darkened church, light spreading in every direction as candles were lit; on the altar in the haze of incense from the thurible and, most importantly of all, in that delicate and heart-stopping removal of the purple cloths from the statues.

The gallery was not the place to be for any of this.

John Vincent Holland and the Racing Boys

My father was the one who told me the story – many times – about the strange man who came back from the Great War and organised races for the young boys in the local park. My father was ten when the Great War ended and he, like a hundred other youngsters in his home town of Athy, County Kildare, was intrigued by the ex-soldier who lived in the big house on the Model Farm.

Yes, he had served in the war but so had hundreds of others from the parish. Dozens had come back maimed or shocked. But this man was different. This was John Vincent Holland V.C. – the holder of that most distinguished of awards. And here he was organising races for the young boys in the park, offering five shillings to the fastest boy on the day and half a crown to the runners-up. And not just once but many, many times.

"The word would spread," my father told me, "that John Vincent was organising races and we'd head for the People's Park as fast as our legs could carry us. And there he'd be, matching us by age and height, putting us into groups, working out the odds the younger boys should have, making everything as fair as possible."

Even then, as young boys, my father and his comrades had seen enough of the war and its effects to know that John Vincent Holland was suffering from shell-shock and that when he wasn't depressed he was elated and the local youngsters were only too happy to compete for his largesse.

They had seen so many other men come home, wounded and maimed; they had seen the curtains drawn and the black ribbons posted on door after door along Barrack Street and Duke Street, Leinster Street and Meeting Lane. They had grown up in the knowledge that the telegram boy was to be feared and that every time he passed a soldier's house without stopping prayers of thanksgiving were said and sighs of relief were breathed by wives and mothers and children.

Athy was an army town. It sent sixteen hundred men to the trenches in the First Worlds War. Eighty-seven of them never returned, lost to bullets and bayonets, to shells and rats, to the madness – inflicted and self-inflicted. Occasionally a coffin came, as some kind of perverted reward, giving one family a grave at which to pray, a place at which to gather, a piece of earth that would be not forever England but forever the final bed where a son or husband or father slept. But these were the exceptions. For many in that small town straddling the river Barrow there was nothing beyond the knock of the telegram boy, perhaps a letter from the chaplain, the official notification of death; the pension book to keep a family supplied with food and a medal around which to build a memory and a pride or bitterness that grew silent in the new and independent Ireland.

My father was a lifelong republican but when he spoke of the men who had died in the Great War, the men whose sons had been his schoolmates; the men whose wives had often fed him as a young boy, after his own mother died; the men he had known on sight and seen marching to the station when they left Athy for England and, eventually, France, he spoke with a reverence and an understanding.

"Athy was a poor town," he'd say. "You could smell the poverty and they had no choice. It wasn't about politics; it was about necessity. And when they came back, it was to a country that didn't want to know what had happened or why. The men who could work did their best to find it, the men that were maimed lived on what little pensions they got."

And some families suffered more than others: the Staffords lost two sons, the Hannons lost two sons and a nephew, the Kellys lost two sons, and the Curtis family lost three sons. The average death rate among young British men was 1.7 per cent of the population in the Great War – in Athy it was 2.5 per cent.

My father often spoke of John Vincent Holland the races and the prize money and how, from time to time, Holland would produce his Victoria Cross and the boys would gather round him in the People's Park and a silence would fall, a recognition – even in childhood – that the medal and the ribbon had been hard won and that the shillings they were racing for were, in their way, blood money, drenched in their fathers' and uncles' and brothers' blood and given to them by a man who, even in his living, had paid too great a price for his survival.

House for Sale

In fairly recent times I've been seriously house-hunting. I've listened to the sages and prophets tell me that it's a buyer's market. I've heard auctioneers tell me that cash is king. I've heard voices in my head – or so it seems – tell me that the market hasn't bottomed out yet. I've heard the European Central Bank tell me there's no money about. I've heard the government tell me to spend, spend, spend and, to my amazement, I've heard the bank say yes to my mortgage application.

And I've done all the hopping and trotting that goes with house-buying. I've read the blurbs and I've seen the inner workings of their linguistic acrobatics. I've learned to interpret the language of the auctioneer – sorry the estate agent, for it seems the auctioneer is a thing of the past. The auctioneer was the man who stood on a barrel in a farmyard to auction the first house I ever tried to buy. I was twenty-four and had scraped, begged and borrowed every penny I could get. I'd cajoled my bank manager into agreeing that I could bid up to £17,000 for a run-down cottage with a large garden on which my heart was set.

I'd even got into the habit of walking every evening the mile and a half from where I was living, and peering in the windows of the cottage, mentally decorating and re-arranging. I think I may even have found a place for the Christmas tree though it was high summer.

And so, on the appointed day, a crowd gathered, the auctioneer climbed onto the barrel in the cottage yard, I positioned myself where I knew my practised nod could be seen and the bidding began with an opening offer of ... £19,000! I was out of the running before the race had even begun. Lesson learned. I don't remember what the house sold for – £27,000 I think

– but I do remember that the auctioneer conducted the lively and intense bidding war with his flies undone.

My more recent outings have been to view properties that have been described in glowing terms in the brochures. But I've learned – as I learned on that summer afternoon thirty-five years ago – that *quaint* often means derelict; *a blank canvas* means the sky is not only your limit but your roof as well; *ideal as a starter home* means the hot-press is probably the biggest room in the house; *detached* can mean that you could possibly, in icy weather, squeeze a pencil between one house and the next; *south-facing gardens* will always have one part that faces south, though it may be the step outside the back door; and *in need of some redecoration* means the rafters are sagging, the walls are not insulated and the windows can't quite contain the freezing air before it escapes to the milder climate outside. A*n ideal project for the DIY enthusiast* means that three of the walls are more or less in place but the septic tank is actually on an adjoining property which, coincidentally, also happens to be for sale – but at twice the price.

All of which is fine – you learn the language and you live with it. But what has amazed me is the way in which auctioneers – oops, sorry, estate agents – now advertise their "properties" on internet sites, with glowing photographs. And how these photos either avoid the obvious deficiencies or flaunt them. Either way, it makes for interesting viewing.

A few recent trips through the on-line property market have thrown up some gems.

One house I looked at had eleven photographs on view – one of the front aspect of a cottage and ten of the large shed to the rear. The accompanying text sang the praises of this spacious and multi-purpose workplace which housed the oil tank, the burner, an office and a workshop, a loo and an assortment of kennels. Who'd need the house – it's a mere afterthought!

Another property had four photographs of the kitchen fridge – including two close ups of the array of fridge magnets with their poems, prayers and promises. All very uplifting but I would really have preferred a view of the room. The same auctioneer had a wonderful photo of a gleaming bidet but nothing about the bathroom which, with any luck, housed it.

A cottage which sounded idyllic materialised, when I reached the photos on-line, with a neo-Romanesque front wall that appeared to have been partially eaten by a marauding, concrete-chewing dinosaur. Or perhaps a truck had gone through it and no one had bothered with the repairs. Given its proximity to a wild range of mountains, the former seemed the more likely explanation. Furthermore – and I think this proves the dinosaur theory – the occupants had obviously fled in terror, leaving in their wake clothes, books, wheel-less prams, empty dog-food cans and three-legged bed frames.

My favourite find was a bungalow that was described on-line as sitting on a meticulously kept plot with new fascia and guttering making it an ideal, "turn-key" purchase. The fact that the house had a radiant front garden of beautifully flowering ragwort was charming and colourful in its own way – but the fact that a healthy alder tree was growing from the newly installed gutter at the back of the house was another thing altogether. When I pointed this out to the auctioneer he said: "Yerra, it shows how good the gutters are, that they didn't come down – not even in the big snow!"

Not surprisingly, the search went on.

I Knew This Place

A Last Supper

I came home from the local hall to the smell of an apple tart baking in the oven. My mother was sitting, as she so often did at that hour of the night, at the kitchen table playing patience.

"Well," she asked, "how did the play go?"

"Great," I said. "We had a full house and people seemed to love it. You'll see for yourself tomorrow night."

It was 1977, late January, and I was in the middle of a run of *The Risen People* with the local drama group. Three nights down, one to go.

"There's an apple tart baking, it's almost done," my mother said, "but you probably won't want it while it's hot."

I've never liked apple tart straight from the oven, just as I've never liked warm scones.

"Thanks. I'll have some tomorrow," I said.

Sometime in the small hours I woke to the sound of the doorbell ringing. By the time I got to the landing, my father was leading our GP up the stairs. A few moments later my father was back downstairs, ringing for an ambulance.

"Your mother is not well," he said.

And then the doctor was with us, standing in the small hall.

"I'll wait till the ambulance arrives," he said. "I've given her an injection. The sooner we get her to hospital the better."

My father nodded and then turned to me.

"You might go up and sit with her while I put on the outside light for the ambulance driver."

In my parents' room my mother lay in bed, her eyes closed.

"How are you feeling?" I asked.

"I have a terrible headache," she whispered.

"Is there anything I can do?"

She smiled a weak smile.

"You might rub some 4711 on my forehead."

I took the small bottle from the bedside locker and rubbed the cologne gently on her temple.

"That's better," she said.

And then the doctor was back in the room and, shortly afterwards, the ambulance arrived and my mother was lifted onto a stretcher and, between the paramedics, my father and myself, we carried her slowly down the narrow stairs and out to the waiting ambulance. My father climbed in beside her and the lights flashed blue as they faded down the bleak street.

"I think your mother may have had a brain haemorrhage," the doctor said as I walked him to his car.

I nodded. I could think of nothing to say.

That evening, when I got home from school, my father had returned from the hospital and he confirmed the news. It wasn't good. My mother had, indeed, had a severe haemorrhage. The prognosis was bleak.

He had prepared dinner, knowing I had to be gone again in an hour for the final night of the play. We ate in silence, my mother's empty chair a reminder of how quickly our lives had changed and how uncertain the future had become.

The meal over, my father went to make some tea and returned from the back kitchen carrying the teapot and the tart my mother had made the night before. He placed it on the table and sat slowly down. We both stared at the perfectly cooked pastry, risen above the deeply filled fruit. Neither one of us spoke. It was as if the cutting and eating of the food would be a sacrilege. The silence seemed to last an age. A blast of cold rain against the window pane finally broke it.

"We could not eat it," my father said. "We could throw it in the bin but I'm not sure your mother would be impressed."

I leaned across and cut two slices and slowly we ate them, a kind of last supper and the first of many meals we would share together in the weeks between that evening and my mother's death a month later. A breaking of bread and hearts.

Mick Murphy, the Last Railwayman

I was twelve years old
and the steps were very high,
schoolbag discarded at the foot;
the summer burn of sun upon my shoulder,
and I was laughing
as I climbed the swaying timber stairs.

From the shadow of the cabin,
Mick Murphy came to meet me.
Sit down now, Johnny boy, and I'll make a cup of tea.
He swung the billy-can low over smoky turf.
I settled on the well-worn seat.
And there's a bar of chocolate to celebrate the day.

On the siding I saw my father uncouple flat-bed trucks,
released for loading at the store.
Lifting his hand, he waved
and I waved back.
Summer sat between us
and this was 1965.

And now, from half a century away,

I turn as I descend those absent steps

and see Mick Murphy lean, shirt-sleeved, out of the window space.

His thumb is lifted in the shining air,

and he calls across the track, *Enjoy the summer, Johnny boy,*

days pass and days are gone before we even know.

Going to the Gaeltacht

In 1964 I was an eleven-year-old, in fifth class in primary school. My mother, herself a teacher, had a passion for the Irish language and she reckoned my Irish was far from *snasta*. And so I was sent to the Connemara Gaeltacht for three months – from January to March of that year. Mind you, I wasn't the only one to hit the road west – two or three others from my village were also sent packing to brush up on the *blas*.

We all landed in the same parish and were deposited in houses where we could go through a process of total immersion. My house had a wonderful and endlessly talkative *bean a' tí*; and a *fear a' tí* who said very little but smiled a lot, and two small boys, aged three and five. It didn't have electricity or running water but it had a really warm welcome and it had a house next door that seemed to have an endless rota of children in and around my own age and they, too, made me welcome and helped me overcome my homesickness.

Not only did the neighbours have electricity – they also had a television, which was more than we had at home – and a place was made for me on the extended settee – which in fact was a brilliantly devised series of car seats which could be added to or subtracted from as the audience demanded. Of course, I wasn't supposed to watch television because the programmes were in English but, as my *bean a' tí* was fond of saying: *Níl aon dochar ann*.

The only danger to my surreptitious and harmless television-watching – which stretched to half an hour, twice a week – was the local Ceannaire, the man on the bike who could (and did) call unannounced to ensure that we were not speaking English, watching television or getting up to any other

52

kind of devilment. Sometimes he'd arrive at the school and each *dálta* would be taken out to the corridor for a quick pep talk and an interrogation. Sometimes, he'd arrive at the house and drink tea and eat bread and jam and talk about me as though I wasn't there and, sometimes, I'd meet him on the road or in the village and he'd stop to ask gruffly how my Irish was improving?

In the second week of February 1964 a wave of excitement washed over the house next door. Word had leaked out that there was to be a film in the local *halla* on the following Friday night and all of the children aged ten and over were going and wouldn't I come too and wouldn't we all have a wonderful time and wasn't this the best thing ever?

Ar agaidh leat, the *bean a' tí* said, *Sure nach bhfuil na lads next door ag dul ann fresin?* The *fear a' tí*, as ever, said nothing at all, just nodded and smiled.

And so it came to pass – Wednesday drifted into Thursday and Thursday into Friday and the excitement was monumental. I went to the *siopa* that afternoon, on my way from school and spent my week's pocket money – all but the admission price – on sweets for all of us. By tea-time we were like hens on a hot griddle and by seven o'clock we were ready to leave, giving ourselves an hour to make the five-minute walk.

We got there in the end, thirty minutes before the film was due to begin, took our seats in the front row and I shared the sweets with my companions. Bit by bit the *halla* filled and by ten to eight the place was full. Had the lights gone out then and the film started none of what happened next might ever have occurred but the lights didn't go out and, somehow or other, the Ceannaire saw me among the children in the front row. Not that I was hiding – as far as I was concerned, there was no reason to hide. But he had other ideas.

He stomped up the aisle, lifted me by the arm from my seat, my sweets scattering across the floor.

Tá bloody hard neck agat teacht isteach anseo was all he said but his voice boomed through the quietened hall as he frog-marched me to the door and pushed me into the darkness outside.

I hung around for a while, humiliated and afraid but, in the end, the cold drove me home to my lodgings. Too embarrassed to tell the truth, I said I didn't feel well. The bean a' tí made hot milk and toast and tucked me into bed.

The following morning, the oldest of the girls from the house next door – she was probably fourteen or fifteen – arrived with my scattered sweets intact and with the truth about what had happened.

The fear a' tí listened, as ever, in silence and then said, very quietly: *Ná bach leis an bpleidche sin, nil ann ach fear beag ar rothar mór.*

I may not have understood the subtleties in what he said but I got the gist and I felt a damn sight better.

Summer

Working on the Railway

When I was in primary school, I'd spend an hour or two every afternoon in the signal cabin waiting for my father to finish work, and then we'd drive the ten-miles home from Athy to Castledermot and he'd talk about the railway. He had worked on the railway for most of his life; his father and brother had worked on the railway and my mother's father and brother had worked on the railway. "There's no denying it," he'd say. "We're a railway family."

By then, my brother was studying medicine and my sister was on her way to becoming a teacher. I was the last possible candidate for railway work.

"You wouldn't have to start at the bottom, like I did," my father would say. "If you had a good education, you could start in the office, as a clerk. You could work your way up to Station Master and Inspector." Inspector was the highest accolade my father could imagine. That would be the top of the tree as far as he was concerned.

"It's a good career and steady. And for a chap like you, with a head on his shoulders, the sky's the limit. If you got a good Leaving Cert, you'd have all the options open to you. It's something you should think about."

At the time, I just wanted to work on the trains. The idea of being stuck in an office held no appeal for an eleven-year-old. Better still, I could be a guard on a goods' train. The guard's van seemed like heaven to me, with its wood-burning stove and burnt-black kettle; the hard wooden bunks; the sandwiches wrapped in newspaper; the door opening onto an exposed platform at the rear; the horizontal steps down; the red and green oil-burning lanterns on the back. It offered everything a boy could want –

freedom, privacy, travel, adventure, responsibility. I had visions of long trips from Dublin to Sligo – the stove burning brightly and the kettle singing while the wind and rain stormed outside. At home, I took over a disused rabbit hutch and hung sacks across the open sides and pretended it was a guard's van. If ever I worked on the railway, I decided, I wanted to be a guard.

"You'd soon grow tired of that," my father would say but I didn't believe him. Who could grow tired of such an escapade. New stations, new people but, most importantly, the solitude in between. I didn't know the word solitude back then, I only knew the word aloneness, but it was that aloneness, that solitude, that isolation that appealed to me.

I was never happier than when I was out walking the dogs, Brandy and Soda, over Rice's Hill, down through the Rocks and out past Halfmiletown. Out there the countryside was deserted – just me and the dogs and my imagination. I dreamt of living in Joe Shea's derelict cottage on the banks of the river Lerr. I spent summer days walking and imagining. Later, in my teens, I walked and imagined and hoped I'd meet some Ruth in search of her redeemer but all I saw was the occasional fisherman, as anxious to avoid me as I was to avoid him.

"Sure, have a think about it," my father would say, as we pulled into the yard at home.

"I will," I'd say.

Years afterwards, I began at last to value my father's dream. He wasn't just interested in seeing me settled in a permanent and pensionable job with prospects. He loved the idea of the family continuing its connection with the railways. His own career had been thwarted as a result of his involvement in a strike and his ambition of becoming a Station Master or an Inspector had never been achieved. His job as Station Foreman in Athy was important to him, and he valued the position, but there was within him that *might have been*, that knowledge that he was intelligent enough and ambitious enough to have made it farther up the ladder but, he believed, his active involvement in the NATE union had stood in his way. I think he saw in me the chance for the family to make an even bigger mark in CIE. But I was to disappoint him and, despite a summer spent working on the permanent way, teaching, my mother's trade, became mine, too, if only for a time. But the allure of the Guard's Van has never faded, even though the vans themselves are long gone now.

Al Fresco

We were sitting at a pavement table outside *The Mad Hatter* restaurant in Castledermot, my friends and myself. The hot summer sun beating down on shoulders, cappuccinos on the table, the slow hum of passing traffic occasionally breaking into our conversation. All was well with the world and the summer stretched lazily ahead of us.

The conversation rambled over the past, over people we had known and things that had happened in the village during the past forty years. And then, in turning to take a milk jug from the table behind me, the sunlight caught the newly painted wall of Cope's shop across the road and, beneath the paint, the outline of the windows that had in recent years been closed up and plastered over.

In that moment, the sun receded and it was suddenly a cold, wet winter afternoon. Darkness had fallen beneath the slanted weight of pouring rain and I was hurrying past Carlow Gate, running against the wind and rain, passing the dim lights of Savage's and MacEvoy's shop windows, crossing the empty Square and rounding the corner of Cope's shop.

Already there were twenty or thirty children packed around the large window, pushing and shoving for a better view of the small, black and white television that sat in the window, surrounded by pots and pans and the other bits and pieces of hardware that were for sale.

Scrambling through the bodies, I found myself a place where the wind and rain were irrelevant, a place where I could clearly see the TV screen. It was half past five, it was a winter Saturday afternoon and Rin Tin Tin was about to enthral the gathered children with another silent black and white adventure. We stood in awe, comments passing, mouths falling open as he raced across the hot desert sands. The rain and cold disappeared and, for that half hour, we were no longer prisoners of our own poverty.

And nor were we the only ones to stand at that window in the rain, watching the silent screen flicker. Later that night, and every Saturday night through the winter, men and women would gather to watch *The Late Late Show*, seeing without hearing the procession of guests being silently interviewed by Gay Byrne. This silent show was their Rin Tin Tin; it drew them from their homes in spite of the weather and held them enthralled. The missing voices, the silent opinions didn't seem to matter. Instead, the wonder of these pictures and the stories that they could build out of the silences were enough to hold their attention and keep them there in spite of wind, rain, frost and snow.

I turned back to my companions and the angled light of the sun shot off our table, the hunched ghosts of those people – my childhood self among them – disappearing into the warm afternoon. I listened to the conversation of my two companions but, every now and then, I glanced across my shoulder at the plastered window space in search of the silent, absent figures who had peopled that spot on winter nights.

Breaking the Rules

I don't remember the exact year but it was definitely pre-Vatican Two and I was an altar boy, the Latin phrases tripping off my tongue as though I understood them. From the *In nomine Patris et Filii et Spiritus Sancti* at the opening of the Mass to the last *Requiem aeternam donna eis, Domine. Et lux perpetua luceat eis* of the *De Profundis*, I was prepared for all eventualities. So, when word came that one of our neighbours had died, I presumed I'd be in line to serve at her funeral Mass.

It was only when my mother sent me up the house of the dead woman with two apple tarts and a dozen scones that I discovered Mrs J was a Protestant and there wouldn't be a Mass. Nor, indeed, would she be left overnight in her own church. Instead, her coffin would leave the house at half past two the following afternoon for a service in St James's Church of Ireland and she'd be buried afterwards in the adjoining graveyard, that ancient space that was our playground in summer, its nineteenth-century table headstones providing us with hiding places for games of Cowboys and Indians. Sometimes, as I lay in the cool darkness beneath a stone, I'd imagine the permanent occupant below me breathing a deep and angry sigh, but I'd put the notion from my head and crouch a little lower to avoid detection.

The following afternoon, I stood with my father at the gate of Mrs J's house and we waited with all the other neighbours for her husband and sons to carry the coffin down the short pathway and slide it into the back of the waiting hearse. And then the cortege moved off and we followed behind. Voices drifted from the crowd around me.

"A lovely woman."

"Oh she was, she was. And quiet."

"You wouldn't know she was there half the time. Kept herself to herself."

"She did."

"And she'll be missed. It'll take himself a while to get over it."

"It will."

"Sure they were inseparable."

"Oh they were, they were."

The procession wound down Abbeylands, through Carlow Gate, then right onto the School Lane and across Main Street onto Church Lane. The round tower pushed its head above the sycamores and the hearse slowed and then halted at the gates of the churchyard. The crowd stood back, waiting for the family to appear, allowing space for them to carry Mrs J's coffin through the yawning gates and then a handful of people followed it up the gravelled path, beneath the Romanesque archway and through the open doorway of the church. I felt my father's hand take mine and lead me through the gateway, following the family and the few Church of Ireland parishioners who had come to say farewell. The rest of the neighbours remained behind, waiting outside the gates until the funeral service would end and they could safely walk to the graveside, free of the sin that entering a Protestant church for a Protestant service would bring crashing down around them.

Inside, my father and I sat on a narrow wooden pew halfway up the church. There were long cushions on these pews, unlike the hard wooden seats to which we were accustomed. And there were soft kneelers when we bent to pray but, mostly, we sat and listened. The words were all in English, though the readings sounded odd.

If ye abide in me and my words abide in you, ye shall ask what ye will and it shall be done unto you. Herein is my father glorified that ye bear much fruit; so shall ye be my disciples.

Afterwards, as we made our way home, an acquaintance of my father's overtook us.

"You'll be bringing the wrath of the PP down on you," he smiled but, even as a child, I recognised the disapproving coldness behind the smile.

"I'll take my chances," my father said and I noticed that his gait had speeded up.

"It'll be one for confession," the man said. The smile was gone now.

"She was a good neighbour in life," my father said. "Why wouldn't I see her off in death. Nothing to confess. Love thy neighbour, was that what Jesus preached?"

At home, my mother said: "Well?"

"Oh the gossips will have their field day," my father growled and then he sat in his favourite chair and slipped off his boots and socks.

"See," he said, "not a sign of a cloven hoof."

And from the back kitchen, I heard my mother laugh.

The Black Dog

It's funny, in its own way, how the black dog comes creeping in the most unlikely places. One recent morning, the sun shining and everything right with the world, I went with a friend to visit a friend of hers. While they chatted, I took off on a ramble with the three-year-old daughter of the house.

I'd met her before and I knew she'd keep me royally entertained; she has the gift of the gab. So, we headed away through the enormous garden – and my small companion pointed out the apple trees; the log-pile; her granddad's shed – which turned out to be a wonderfully stocked greenhouse; the big wood – which revealed itself as half a dozen trees at the edge of the lawn – and on down to where a mare, her foal and an instantly friendly donkey were grazing in the river field.

No question went unanswered and no flower was beneath consideration. We floated sticks in the small river; we built a pebble house; we brought carrots to the donkey and we closed and opened and closed and opened the gate at the top of the drive a half-dozen times.

And all the while the sun shone and the sky was blue and we laughed a lot. No sign of the black dog anywhere; no shadows on the grass; no shape in the undergrowth; no reflection in the low, clear water; not a hint of a bark between the songs of the swooping birds.

We wound our way to a neat, compact glasshouse on the edge of the orchard and my small companion showed me the rows of strawberries, still green and hard.

"They grow at night," she whispered, confidentially. "When we're asleep."

I nodded.

"And one night they go red and then I can eat them. That's what granddad said."

Suddenly, her words were like a disappearing voice and I was conscious of the black dog's sneaking presence. I neither saw nor heard him but I smelled his smell and felt that awful tiredness at the back of my eyes, that giveaway sensation that lets me know for sure when he's about. Not that he always smells the same – in fact he can disguise himself in almost any smell – childhood sweets; a perfume from some almost forgotten but suddenly recovered night; orange peel slowly burning in a dying fire; the lilac of early summer or, as in this case, the warm smell of summer earth. And, of course, those smells most often come without his stalking close behind – they mostly come, presaging only the season or the flower or the sunshine memory of a day in childhood or a night in love.

But, when the black dog's shadow falls, it crashes with the heaviness of a stone wall collapsing. In that warm, well-kept glasshouse, the little girl suggested we close our eyes to see if the strawberries might think we were asleep and ripen and be ready to eat. But I knew, if I closed my eyes, that the weight of the shadow would make it almost impossible for me to open them again. And around me the voices and the scents and the fleeting, spectral images of other children – my own children – were running and skipping and laughing and racing – but in the darkness and echo of the fallen shadow – reminding me (as if I need reminding) that life could have been more positive; I could have been kinder; could have made a better hand of that most uncertain and unpredictable of jobs, parenthood.

My black dog comes without calling; comes in his own time and at his own pace and I'm never certain quite what it is that attracts him. Is it those certain smells that resurrect him? Is it a particular photograph; a recovered memory; a word here; something glanced in passing; the presence of one child and the absence of another? I have no idea.

All I know is that he has this ability to get under the skin, to infiltrate the heart and mind; to dim the soul and generate great doubt and enormous disappointment in the self. In that moment, standing with my little companion, in the bright, warm glasshouse, barely hearing her words and her laughter, I would have wished for her a life beyond such falling shadows, a life well clear of black dogs and dark though sunlit days. But I didn't have the energy to wish these wishes, though now – of course – I do.

For myself there could only be the deep, accepting draw of breath that comes in the wake of the shadow falling; the inevitability of the days ahead; the lack of energy and purpose; the bones that ache; the voice that says to stay in bed; to stay indoors; to avoid all human contact, the voice that wants only its own companionship, the dismal hermit.

That's what the black dog brings but then – eventually – he goes away again, slipping into the night; becoming a shape remembered; a shadow thrown; a weight recollected behind the eyes, a welcome absence one morning.

The summer stretches ahead and we open our eyes – my small companion and I – to find that the night has passed and the strawberries are a deep and luscious red.

Home Thoughts from Abroad

I was looking for something recently and it set me rereading the great English poet John Clare and that, in turn, had me thinking on his reflection that "anticipation is the sweetest of earthly pleasure."

How true it is – or was – particularly where music was concerned.

Today, if I want to hear a piece of music, even one that's never been released, I can Google the title or search on YouTube and, likely as not, I'll find it in seconds. Which is a wonderful facility but it comes without the sweetness of which John Clare wrote – the sweetness of anticipation.

It was a Saturday afternoon. I remember that clearly. And it was in the July of 1973.

I was driving from Castledermot to Athy and, just as I passed through the village of Kilkea – no let me be more specific – just as I passed the church in Kilkea, I heard the song on the radio, on "Airs and Races."

It was a slow song and a beautiful song and the singer's voice was like nothing I'd ever heard before. I had no idea who he was or what the song was called. All I knew was that I loved it the moment I heard it, loved it so much that I found myself driving more and more slowly until, finally, I pulled into the open gateway of a summer field and heard the song through to its last fading notes, praying there'd be a back-announcement. And there was.

Val Joyce talked about the record, about how wonderful it was and then he named the song – "Home Thoughts from Abroad" – and the singer – a man with the unusual name of Clifford T Ward.

I scrabbled in the dashboard pocket and, finding a pencil, I scrawled the names of the singer and the song on an out-of-date railway ticket.

Half an hour later I was in the record shop on Duke Street in Athy, that shop with its welcoming scrubbed floorboards; its bins of exotic albums; its magic smell of timber and cardboard and vinyl; that shop where an hour's browsing might turn up some new gem. It was there that I bought Jethro Tull's *Heavy Horses* purely because the title intrigued me. It was there I first heard Dan Hill and there I bought a Chopin album simply because I liked the sleeve.

But on this Saturday afternoon there was no browsing. Instead, I went straight to the counter and pulled the train ticket from my pocket.

"I'm looking for a song called "Home Thoughts from Abroad." The singer is a guy called Clifford T. Ward."

The shop assistant shook her head. There was no computerised list to check and, besides, she didn't need to. She knew every album and single in stock.

"I can get it for you," she said. "I can get it for you on Thursday in Dublin."

"Great."

"If it's an LP, do you want that or just the single?"

"The LP, please."

She wrote the song title in her order book.

"What's the guy's name again?"

"Clifford T. Ward."

"I'll have that for you on Friday."

Friday was almost a week away but the alternative was to drive to Dublin and I couldn't do that. My father wouldn't give me the car for a journey that would, in his opinion, be perilous beyond my driving ability and, anyway, I was working Monday to Friday as a labourer on the permanent way for CIE!

So wait I must.

I knew that the record shop owner travelled to Dublin every Thursday –
a half-day in the town of Athy – with a list of LPs and singles that had been
ordered – and I knew that once the shop opened, on Friday morning, the
record would be there, or not, depending on its availability. The
anticipation of hearing the song; of seeing what this singer looked like; of
listening to the other songs on the LP, if LP there were – and I couldn't be
sure of even that much – meant the week ahead would be filled with
excitement.

No instant access, no checking YouTube, just a week of work and
waiting until the next weekend when, again, I'd be in the record shop.

And, sure enough, there was the album, waiting for me, the following
Saturday afternoon. With its sepia photograph of a long-haired man with
wide eyes and an honest face. And when I got it home I listened, enthralled,
to the songs he had written, their beauty heightened by the sense of
anticipation I'd revelled in all week long. And most of all I listened to the
title track with its references to Keats and Robert Browning.

Years later, I would interview Clifford T. Ward. He was ill by then and
singing was no longer a possibility for him so, instead, he talked about
"Home Thoughts from Abroad" and the things that had inspired it. And I
told him the story of how I'd first heard it and how I'd waited patiently for
its arrival, and we laughed. And the wonderful thing was that it was still as
breath-taking and beautiful a song as it ever had been and all that waiting
had been so well worth the effort.

Keats and Browning and Clifford T. Ward and, of course, John Clare –
Anticipation, the sweetest of earthly pleasures.

John MacKenna

Lilac Time

We moved house in July 1958 – all the way from one side of the football field in Castledermot to the other; from the Low Terrace to the High Terrace; from a small enclave of less than two dozen cottages with enormous gardens to a row of more recently built, two storeyed houses. All that summer day we crossed and re-crossed the football field, our furniture going in one direction, the furniture of the family with whom we'd swapped going in the other. I was five years old and my contribution can't have been very great.

Once we'd settled into the new house, the work began – redecoration started with fresh coats of paint on every room. Over the following months and years, a back kitchen was built; a garage was erected; a new front wall was constructed; the garden was taken in hand.

It must have been two or three years later, when all the essential work had been done, that my mother decided she would like a lilac tree in the garden. The shrub was bought and my memory is that Mrs O'Connell from next door, herself a keen and talented gardener, was involved in the consultations and discussions that went on over several evenings. I remember my father eventually giving up on moving and removing the lilac tree and informing my mother and Mrs O'Connell that when they finally decided on a location, he'd be happy to get the spade from the shed and plant it but that there was a garden to be dug, drills to be made and potatoes to be sown and, in the meantime, he'd leave them to it. Eventually, a site was agreed and the lilac was planted at the end of the trellis that divided our backyard from O'Connell's.

But that lilac was to prove a huge disappointment to my mother. It grew,

70

tall and strong and, come early summer each year, its leaves unfurled and its branches spread against the new blue sky. It was healthy and green, rising vigorously year after year but never flowering. Each May into June, my mother would inspect the new growth, searching for a sign of a purple flower but, to her great frustration, none ever appeared.

In 1970, when I sat my Leaving Cert, the lilac in the school grounds in Limerick was bent low with flowers, their deep, rich scent filling the air of the common room where we students spent our time between exams. I remember telling my mother about it when I got home.

"It'll never happen here," she said wistfully, her eyes fixed on the broad high branches of her own lilac tree, its opaque green leaves dancing in the early summer breeze, their emerald and olive seeming to mock her.

And so that tree stood and flourished in our garden through every spring of the nineteen sixties and into the seventies, forever green but never producing a single lavender or mauve petal.

In February 1977 my mother died. We buried her on a bitterly cold afternoon when spring was nothing more than a word and February was holding firmly to the coat tails of winter. The only flowers in her garden were snowdrops and even the ditches in the fields behind the house showed not even a hint of the first primroses or wild violets.

And then, one morning in late May of that year, Mrs O'Connell called me from her back garden.

"There's something you should see," she said and her voice was warm and high with excitement.

We walked side by side, one on each side of the wooden trellis that still divided our gardens.

"Look," she said. "Just look." And a broad smile lit her face, a smile of wonder, a smile that hinted at something beyond the ordinary.

The broad expanses of the lilac branches that had grown and spread along the line between our gardens for sixteen years were packed with parcels of unopened purple flower, still dark but unlocking into the lighter shades of plentiful sweetness. We stood, each on our own side of the tree, and marvelled at this strangeness, this flowering that had come out of the blue. And in the days and weeks that followed, the lilac fully bloomed, its bountiful blossoms filling the garden with their rich perfume that said *summer*, that said *warmth*, that said *life*, that said *was I not well worth waiting for?*

Brian's Music

(*for Brian Hughes*)

It comes in waves that break,
it slides between the silences,
it values hesitation
like a single feather from a circling bird –
is this not what we mean when we talk of *spiorad naofa*?

Táimse im Chodladh; *The Primrose Lass*;
The Dirty Trettles and *The Pleasures of Hope* -
names skip like dancing shoes;
Lazarus tunes that bring the dead to life
for one more round of the kitchen floor.

Melodies that open every lock along the Grand Canal,
refrains that shelter in the lee of winter trees
pushed low with snow, gone hard with frost;
revealing spring on quiet roads;
bent lower, still, with apples in the glory days.

When Brian puts the timber to his lips
high larks fall shy, astonished by the sound
that brings a thousand years of living and of death
together in one place, one time,
in the music of one man...

The Record Player

The record player had arrived one Christmas Eve – with a handful of borrowed LPs -- Mario Lanza's *The Student Prince*; *The Sound of Music*; two collections of Christmas carols. As far as I remember, it came with my brother from Dublin, arriving on the late train. And, as far as I remember, the LPs were borrowed from Frank McDonald, our singing butcher, who went on to be a fine actor in Dublin's Focus Theatre and in film and on tv. But, in the mid-sixties, he was still our butcher, appearing in local opera productions by night, parcelling chops and liver by day.

The record player was a run of the mill, mono box with the three speeds – 78, 45 and 33⅓. And that's important because the story I'm about to tell you has very little to do with Christmas or late trains or borrowed LPs. The story I'm about to tell you comes from a warm summer afternoon about four years after the arrival of the record player. By then someone – and it may have been me but I'm not prepared, even at this remove, to admit it – had damaged the arm of the record player so that it skipped and bounced like a stone across water. But, necessity being the mother of most things, I had sellotaped a halfpenny to the top of the arm and the weight kept the needle from jumping. It didn't do the needle much good and it wasn't the best thing for records but it worked and, when you're fifteen, tomorrow is a long time.

In October 1968, I asked my mother if I could have a guitar for my birthday – it seemed like a good idea at the time. By then, I'd spent five years taking piano lessons and could play simple tunes, very slowly – *adagissimo* was the term I liked to use – it means very slowly – oh and I could play right hand only. And, ideally, in fact essentially, the pieces needed to be in the key of C. And I had to have the music in front of me!

But the guitar looked a lot more manageable. A couple of the lads in school played guitar and, as far as I could see it was (a) very easy; (b) a lot handier to carry than a piano and (c) a magnet for girls. And in the multiple choices that was my life as a fifteen-year-old, (c) was the oft-desired but seldom achieved answer to most things.

So the guitar arrived and I discovered that not only could I not play it, I couldn't even tune it. Eight months of cut fingers, attempted chord changes and total frustration reminded me of something I had taken five years to learn on a piano stool – I can't, never could and never will be able to really play an instrument.

By the time the summer holidays arrived, I was no further along the musical road than I had been the previous autumn. But ... and here's the important point...there was now a girl on the scene. Let me clarify: as far as I was concerned she was on the scene, the fact that she knew nothing about this was a minor matter. She lived four doors up the road and I was anxious to make an impression on her. We'll call her Kathleen, which is what her family called her, too.

It seemed to me that music would be the language of love and that if she thought I could sing and play the guitar, she might consider going to the pictures with me or going for a walk or...even talking to me. I also knew that she passed my house most evenings on her way home from her summer job. So the plan was hatched. I had a Paul Simon album on which he sang one song with just a simple guitar backing and I, in my naivety and desperation, thought that if I sat outside the sitting-room window – guitar in hand – with the record player hidden behind the curtain, and waited until I saw her turning the corner at the end of the road, reached in and put the needle in the groove, she'd be impressed by *my* singing and *my* playing as she passed.

And on that bright summer evening everything went to plan. As Kathleen turned the corner, I slipped the needle onto the album, track 2 – *Leaves That Are Green* – duration 2 minutes 41 seconds – not too long, not too short. And away we went, Paul Simon and myself. Me picking silently at my guitar strings, he working away behind the curtain. And along came Kathleen, walking quickly then more and more slowly, dawdling past our wall, clearly impressed.

But, just as I got to the second verse – the one that goes: *Once my heart was filled with the love of a girl, I held her close but she faded in the night*, my beautiful rendition suddenly accelerated into a version by the Chipmunks and Kathleen's expression turned from surprise to derision and she burst out laughing and went her merry, skipping way, throwing me a pitying glance as she turned in the gateway of her house, her head shaking, my chances fading in the blood-coloured light.

Behind me, through the open window, I heard my brother laugh, "It's all a game of turelumbuk, the more you put down, the less you pick up" and then he slid the speed back to 33 and Paul Simon went on singing.

But by then I was on my way back inside, my guitar under my arm, my musical career in tatters, my love, as Neil Diamond would note years later, on the rocks.

Marrying Nan Kinsella

I still remember the day I married Nan Kinsella. I had known her for as long as I could remember and she'd known me all my life – literally. Hadn't her mother and herself done a quick tidy up before the doctor and midwife arrived at the house to deliver me!

She lived just three doors from us on the Low Terrace and when my mother returned to teaching, a couple of weeks after my birth, Nan and her mother were to take it in turns to come and look after me in the house. But the story my mother told had a different twist to it.

The Kinsellas were never early to bed or early to rise. It was touch and go whether their lights or ours were last out in the early hours of the morning. The result was that Nan or her mother would arrive to mind me as my mother left for school but, once my mother was out of sight, they'd take me across the road to their own house. Then, at ten to three, Nan and her mother or a couple of her sisters would descend on our house, give it a quick once-over, get the fire going and await my mother's arrival.

That lasted for a while until the pretence was dispensed with and my mother would drop me to Kinsella's on her way to work. Once I learned to walk, I'd toddle over myself before my mother was even out the door. From the time I was three, Kinsella's was the sanctuary I'd run to when I was in trouble. And another great thing was that I didn't have to take my shoes off at their door!

Kinsella's back garden – unlike our own – wasn't tilled and the long grass was a wilderness where I could get safely lost on summer afternoons, sometimes chasing the elusive elephants that Nan told me lived near the ditch into the Cavalry field. In wintertime, on bitter days when my mother wouldn't dream of letting me out, Nan and myself would set off on adventures across the snowy wastes of the Arctic garden. "Risking life and limb," Nan would say. I didn't quite know what that meant but I knew it was worth doing. We'd skate on the frozen dyke at the garden's end or venture out onto the endless whiteness of the football field, unsure we'd ever find our way back home. When the rains came, we'd make a tent and camp under the kitchen table and Nan would borrow her brother Harry's bicycle lamp and steal biscuits from the tin in the bottom cupboard and we'd forget the world outside.

In the summer of my fifth year I married Nan Kinsella. She was thirty-seven. The ceremony was held in Kinsella's garden and she looked more beautiful than I'd ever seen her look before. She wore a bright summer dress and her brown hair fell over her shoulders and she carried a bouquet of wild flowers that she'd picked herself and tied with twine. Her mother was the priest and we repeated words after her and Nan said *I do* and then I said *I do* and afterwards Nan took two apple tarts from the oven and she put a birthday candle on one and lit it.

"Now," she said, "there's a fine wedding cake."

I blew out the candle and she cut the tart and we ate a slice each and drank a glass of lemonade, sitting on the backdoor step. And the sky was blue, even after the sun had gone down. And, because it was summer, I didn't have to go back home until very, very late. And when I did, my new wife walked through the twilight of the low terrace, to my own front door.

But a wedding is not a marriage and a day is not a life and, a few weeks after this, Nan followed her sisters to Birmingham to work, to a city, a country and a life I know nothing about. And that September I went back to school.

From time to time, over the years, we'd meet and chat and laugh and she'd tell me why she'd never married in England. "How could I?" she'd laugh. "Haven't I a husband here?"

And then, in October 2007, an envelope dropped through my letterbox. Inside was an order of service for a requiem Mass in Erdington Abbey Church for Ann Kinsella. And the closing song on that order of service was *Pal of my Cradle Days*.

Indeed, I thought...indeed...

The Last Corncrake

It was a morning in the summer of 1978. For whatever reason, I was up and about just after dawn and I took the dog off for a ramble over the fields – nothing unusual in that. Across the Little River – a stream that can be negotiated in a stride but where, as children, we had fished for pinkeens. On we went, along the banks of the river Lerr, its clear water catching the earliest rays of the stretching sun.

This is the river where, as children, we had tried – in November – to catch trout in sacks. Wading into the two-foot depth of freezing water, we had used an improvised net, made from a coal sack and a length of wire, and tried to lure the unseen brown fish from the overhang of the bank into our badly designed and totally ineffective trap. An hour later all we'd caught were colds.

But on this morning the river was already warm with the season. A light mist hung over the water at the Back River, a dammed three-foot-deep pool where, as a ten-year-old, I had tried, unsuccessfully, to master the art of swimming. Thirty years would pass before I would manage a dozen tentative strokes.

On we went, the dog nosing ahead of me, drawn by the elusiveness of rabbits and foxes, through The Rocks – a sprawling wilderness of granite boulders, furze bushes, reeds and secret hiding places where cowboys camped and Indians laid ambushes for them. The place where one of my childhood friends was stripped to his shorts and staked out, by a warring tribe who promptly forgot all about him, so that, by the time his brothers found him, dehydrated and terrified in the late afternoon, he was severely sunburned.

Crossing the stone bridge at Halfmiletown, we looped back onto the Barrack Road, passing the Mill Pond – drained now but once a place where the serious swimmers went. The same pond where, as a three-year-old, I was placed in a tin bath by my, supposedly, sensible brother and his friends and sent out to sail at the end of a thirty-foot rope on the deep, black waters. Fear or fascination kept me still and, eventually, the tin bath was hauled in and we all went home. When I told my mother about the great adventure, the ructions began in earnest. Even my father, usually the mildest of men when it came to dealing with his children, was less than amused. I couldn't understand the fuss – hadn't my brother and his friends told me I was the lucky one, chosen to sail across the Mill Pond in a tin bath, something never done before.

But, on that early summer morning the tin bath, the heavy jute sack, the days of pinkeen fishing were long, long gone. I was teaching by then, in the local vocational school. Teaching children who had themselves swapped the fascination with pinkeens and fishing and adventures in the Rocks for the lure of the Friday night hop in the youth club and the sound of Blondie, Bob Marley and Showaddywaddy.

On we went, the dog and myself, down into the village and back home. The sun was well clear of the horizon by then, the shadow of the house lay stretched on the lawn between the rose bushes. The dog rambled ahead of me, into the backyard, in search of water and food. I stood at the gate, watching the last of the mist evaporate above the lazy fields.

And then I heard it, the deep, raspy sound of a corncrake coming from somewhere out on Murphy's farm. Distant but not too distant, there like a lure, like a rainbow – always just across the next ditch or the next fence, always within reach, always beyond touch. I knew well enough not to set off in search of the bird, I knew well enough to stand and listen to the raw, throaty song that went on and on across the open sky. What I didn't know was that I would never hear that song again, that the corncrake would never reprise his music in that part of Kildare, that I was privileged to hear what I was hearing.

Like so many other things in life – pinkeen fishing, tin-bath sailing, cowboy and Indian adventures – there comes a day when we step away, without knowing that we will never go back, we become that *Someone* of whom Denis O'Driscoll wrote.

But on that summer morning we shared something, the corncrake and myself. A last song, a few moments of sunlight when the world was ours alone, a farewell that went unrecognised and, as a result, unacknowledged and uncelebrated.

Sorrel

Was there ever a taste that spoke more eloquently or earthily of summer than that of sorrel?

I'm not talking about the garden variety but the wild sorrel plant that was the slaker of thirsts in the sun-drenched fields of childhood.

And thirst was a constant companion in those days – no cans or plastic bottles to drink from; no sachets of fruit juice – just a good swallow of water before you left home. There were a few mothers who insisted that their offspring brought milk or brown sauce bottles of water, with paper stoppers, *just in case*, but inevitably the bottles were stored under a bush or in the long grass, for collection on our return from the wilds beyond the village.

Setting off from home on an adventure meant leaving at nine in the morning and heading back when the six o'clock angelus bell tolled across the parish, calling us to prayer and, more importantly, to food.

Provisions were few – there might be half a Flash bar, a melted Trigger bar or a furry lump of toffee unearthed from the depth of someone's pocket – but these would be gone by the time the fence at the garden's end had been climbed.

What we did have was a solid faith in the earth – a belief that it, like the Lord, would provide in times of need.

Never mind that the stolen apples were stone hard; never mind that the carrots foraged from the long back gardens of rural cottages were pencil thin; never mind that a potato stalk would provide only small spuds for roasting over the open fire; never mind that the waters of the Lerr were uncertain, depending on where you drank along its course – it was the sorrel that tasted of summer.

And it still does, still has that strange power to bring the memories tripping off the tongue. It's acidic tang may have quenched our thirsts way back when but it also proved itself a storehouse of remembering.

I put a leaf on my tongue, I chew it, the bitter taste brings the sun out, brings the feeling of long grass brushing short-trousered, sun-tanned legs; brings the occasional nettle sting as we crossed some ditch from one field to another; brings the soothing coolness of dock leaves on the wounded skin; brings the wobble of stepping stones that constantly threatened to dump us in the eighteen inches of transparent blue water.

It brings the exotic into view – the Big Rock on Rice's Hill from which the valley was surveyed for troops of cavalry who might attack our Apache tribe; the Cuckoo Steps that led us out into Mullarney and the sound – maybe even the sight – of the bird for whom they were named; the Dairy Lane which gave us our first taste of home-grown poetry – *butther and crame from the dairy lane*; the Back River and the Rocks; Crop Hill; Reilly's sandpit; Fraughan Hill and Mullaghcreelan; Skenagun and Ballyvass and out onto the Big Bog – the names and places stumble now like old men in sudden sunlight.

It brings the sounds across the remembered fields and ditches that have been bulldozed one into another – the quarrelling of birds; the rumbling heaviness of bees; the tribal yell of chiefs and braves; the other tribal call of a mother at the foot of some garden below us, shouting a vain reminder about something or other to a child already lost within the circle of a daisy chain; the cry of *Bull! There's a bull behind ya*; the rattling sound of a gate cleared at speed.

I place the sorrel on my tongue; I bite into its sharpness and I know there has never been a taste that spoke more eloquently of childhood and the summer sun.

Summer Table

My mother was sitting on the cemetery wall,
reciting an old poem, not loudly but with the carefulness of one
who knows her discourse might be heard.
Her legs were dangling in the summer air.
The cherry trees had stretched themselves
as far as evening would allow.

That's when she got the news about her son.
I can't be sure who brought the word – that angel of the Lord? –
or if it simply blew in on a western breeze
and landed like a small, dead bird there on her aproned lap.
But, anyway, that's where and when the news arrived.

She dawdled for a moment, the verses hollow now.
Then, finally and silently, traversed the broken ground,
and froze my singing father with her words.
Their eldest child was gone. Softly, they set about preparing
a place for him at the table they had laid.

Heaven's Gate

My father is roller-skating inside the barn. Music rises and falls, wild and wonderful fiddle music. My father loves dancing, he has danced all his life, collecting trophies as he's gone. But I've never seen him roller-skate before and for a man in his hundred and fifth year he's doing really well. His legs are slightly bent and he leans into the air, feet barely leaving the wooden floor, open coat flying behind him as he careers anti-clockwise – round and round, eyes shining with the beauty of it all.

He's doing a thousand times better than I'd ever do. And Kris Kristofferson is sitting on the bleachers watching him, hands joined across his knees, that laconic grin on his bearded face. But my father pays him no heed. He just goes on roller-skating, round and round the beautiful barn with its enormous wood-burning stove and its low, beamed roof. And David Mansfield is playing his fiddle and the music is pouring out, loud and fast and slow and sad, washing like a summer breeze and a winter storm on a deserted American plain.

"It's all about balance," my father shouts quickly as he passes, the words floating over his shoulder with their own perfect poise.

Easy for you to say, I think to myself, easy to skate and talk and laugh and dance when you're a hundred and four years old and dead as a western ghost town. But my father doesn't care.

Then, one by one the actors and the extras and the ghosts of gunfighters and the beautiful women in their long nineteenth century dresses and the men in their bowlers and Stetsons and immigrant caps pour out onto the floor and join my father in this dance of life, love and memory, their faces glowing with the astonishment of pleasure, with the freedom, laughter and carelessness of joy.

And the strange thing is it could be true because I'm standing in the main gallery of VISUAL in Carlow town but I'm not. I'm standing in the barn from Michael Cimino's film *Heaven's Gate* which has been rebuilt by artist Brian Duggan and his team for Eigse Carlow. The project is called "Everything Can Be Done in Principle" and it opened its doors and skating floor to the public just yesterday. The barn is actually here – the music, the skaters, the living and dead will dance and sing. shimmy and weave here in the days and weeks and months of this long summer. They'll come and dress in the costume of the period and strap on their skates and take to the floor and my father's ghost will be among them. And I know why.

He and I only ever went to two films together – one was *Soldier Blue,* and that was the night the chimney went on fire and we found my mother pale-faced and shaken when we got back home. The other was *Heaven's Gate.* And we saw both in the cinema in Carlow – the picture house as my father called it.

We're driving home the last few miles, down the steep descent into Castledermot that night in the early nineteen eighties and my father says quietly: "There's an odd thing now...."

"What's that?" I ask.

"We're coming down Barn Hill," he smiles.

And so we are, past Dempsey's, on the steep descent to Farrelly's bicycle shop.

"Wasn't that a great scene in the picture," he says, "the one in the barn, all those people dancing, all that happiness."

"Even if it didn't last," I add because I didn't inherit his optimism.

"Nothing lasts," my father says, "but sure we have the now. That's where we live."

"Did you like the film?"

"It was a bit slow but I thought that skating scene was wonderful. I wouldn't mind giving that a crack sometime."

"Really?"

"Ah yeah, sure why not? It'd be like dancing only faster, and like running only easier. It'd be great gas altogether."

So here I am, watching my father's ghost, warmed by the smile on his face, cooled by the breeze of the passing skaters, my heart singing its own broken song to David Mansfield's music. I turn for a moment and I catch Kris Kristofferson's eye and he nods towards my skating father and winks and smiles that laconic smile again and I know it's true – everything is possible...in principle.

The Boatman's Story

All day, while the boat slowly circled the island, the Captain had fed us stories about the local history while his wife fed us wonderfully fresh food. The tales were of John the Hermit, who had constructed his own church on the barren side of the island and forbidden women to come near it; of the 18th century landowner who spent thirty years building a dry-stone wall across the mountain for no better reason than to lay claim to half the land and who had died two weeks after finishing what had become his life's obsession; of the Nazi occupation during the Second World War; of the lighthouse towering above us on the edge of a crumbling cliff.

I had gleaned from him, during one of the swimming stops – while we both sat on the boat watching the bathers float through the deep and crystal waters – that his day-job was as a teacher in the island school and his summer job – seven days a week – was taking people round the island on six-hour tours. In the evenings he took the boat out again for sunset cruises.

"You work hard," I said. "Between the teaching and this summer job."

"I had hoped to retire next year," he said, "but I need to teach for five more years to get a reasonable pension. Then my wife and I would like to travel. To be the tourists ourselves."

Before we had a chance to talk any more, the swimmers climbed back onto the boat, the engine came quietly alive and our journey continued.

Two hours later, as the voyage neared its end, the Captain pointed to a tiny church high on the side of a wooded hill that rose above us. I caught only some of what he said and, not wanting to interrupt his story-telling, I didn't question him. But the few phrases I had caught had piqued my interest.

Later that evening, I returned to the harbour but the Captain and his boat were out on a sunset cruise. I waited. Sometime later the boat rounded the sea wall and tied up beneath the clock tower. One by one the evening travellers disembarked until, finally, the Captain was alone.

I stepped onto the boat. He smiled, recognising me from the earlier voyage.

"You spoke about the little church on the wooded hill," I said. "You mentioned a fire and boys. I'm sorry, I didn't hear the rest."

He motioned me to sit opposite him.

"It was 1985," he said. "Difficult times for Greece, much like these times. Three young boys from the town walked out to the little church. Their intention was to take the icons and sell them, to help feed their families. There are more than three hundred churches on the island. They believed there were more than enough icons already in the churches, that the icons from that little place would not be missed."

I nodded.

"They broke into the church and removed the icons. As they left they were confronted by a wildfire which had spread through the trees around the church. They believed their best chance of survival was to run down the hill, towards the sea. They thought the water would be their saviour."

He paused for a moment.

"But they didn't reach the sea," he said. "They were burned in the fire. All three were lost"

"But the church survived."

"Yes, the church survived. If they had stayed there they would have been safe. So every time I pass that church with my boat and my tourists I tell that story. It is part of the island's history. A sad part but not to be forgotten."

And then there was little else to say. I rose, shook his hand and thanked him. As I was about to step from the boat back onto the harbour he laid a hand on my shoulder. I turned. There were tears in his eyes.

"One of those boys was my best friend," he said quietly. "That is my reason for never forgetting, that is why I need to tell the story every day. Because he was my friend – a wild boy, but my friend."

The Boat Boy's Story

He was there every morning, checking tickets, helping people onto the small boat. And he was there every evening, performing the same tasks as we boarded the boat again, for the return journey from the other side of the island to the town harbour. He was a tall young man, fifteen or sixteen years of age, filling his summer holidays with these work days on the boat.

His English was halting but he did his best and it was certainly better than my Greek.

One morning we boarded the boat quite early. The young man hardly bothered to check our tickets. He seemed bothered, jumpy even. And then it appeared, the small parcel. Someone had collected it from the Post Office, brought it down to harbour and delivered it to the young sailor.

He sat in the shelter offered by the awning of the boat, unwrapping the package. The envelope was carefully opened and it revealed a small cardboard box. This, in turn, revealed three rounds of bubble-wrap. Finally, the treasure appeared. It was a wrist watch with a silver band. The young man slipped it onto his wrist, spent a couple of minutes resetting the time and making whatever other adjustments were required – and there appeared to be many – before showing it proudly to the boat's captain and several of the local passengers.

It needed to have one of the links in the wristband removed but, the young man assured me, that would be done by the jeweller on the street by the monastery. He had already worked for seven weeks on the boat, he told me, saving all his money to buy the watch. He had seen it advertised online. Just the week before, he had sent the money to an address in Athens and then waited for the all-important package to arrive in the post. And here it was at last. Tomorrow the jeweller would remove the link and it would fit perfectly.

There was something new in the way he extended his arm to help people on board that morning – now it was the left rather than the right arm, the watch glimmering and glistening in the high, hot sun. The gesture may have meant little to those coming on board but to the young man this was a way of affirming his place in the world. He was no longer a schoolboy, he was a working man, earning a wage, and with a bright new wristwatch to prove it.

That evening, as we embarked, he offered his hand and the watch gleamed again, this time in the setting sun.

The following morning the watch was gone. I assumed he had dropped it to the jeweller's shop or forgotten it in the morning rush to get to the harbour on time for the first sailing. But it didn't appear the following morning either and his wrist remained watch-free for the rest of the week.

On the Saturday evening, as we disembarked, I remarked on the fact that I hadn't seen him wear the watch all week.

"No," he said sadly. "It will not tell time. It will not do anything."

"Have you taken it to the jeweller?"

"Yes, he says it is fake, it is …" He pointed toward the dustbin on the harbour.

"Can you get your money back?"

He shook his head slowly.

"I send cash," he said.

Suddenly, he was a schoolboy again and I remembered a time when I was eleven and I saw an advertisement in the back of a comic for x-ray glasses that allowed you to see people as skeletons. *Amaze your friends with this exciting new insight into the working of the human frame,* the ad said. *Become an expert on human anatomy*, it said.

When the glasses arrived, what I found was a flimsy pair of cardboard spectacles – one red eyepiece, one green – which were, of course, useless. They were probably recycled 3 D glasses

One of my friends tried them on, threw them disparagingly back to me and laughed, *Ya were codded, ya eejit*.

He hadn't needed to tell me, I already knew, and the young boy on the boat didn't need me to tell him. In a day, he had unlearned hope and come face to face with the disappointment and disillusion that are so often the harbingers of adulthood.

Wire Fences Make Good Neighbours

I was teaching a class recently on the poetry of Robert Frost and one of the poems we read and discussed was "Mending Wall" with its line about good fences making good neighbours. And that got me thinking about the wire fences that divided the front and back gardens of the houses on the Low Terrace in Castledermot. The Low Terrace was officially Abbeylands but there were three Abbeylands in the village, all County Council estates but built at differing times, and so, in our childish shorthand, they became the Low Terrace, the High Terrace and the Middle Terrace.

The fences between the gardens on the low and middle terraces were concrete posts with three ribbons of wire looping from post to post. Ideal for children like us to slip between, moving – as we did – from one garden to the next, in search of companionship, or scallions through which to drink water from milk bottles, or potatoes to roast over camp fires, or cabbage stalks with which to whip each other's legs as we refought the Battle of Clontarf.

But later, long after I'd left that class on Robert Frost's poetry, I though more of those fences and of the people who shared them, the adults who rubbed along with each other and allowed that little cul-de-sac to be a place of safety for all of us.

I thought of my parents who kept our garden filled with vegetables and flowers and of the little patch of wilderness at the garden's end where their stillborn children were buried. I thought of Jack and Vera Hickey, next door on one side, and the music of the rosary flooding from their kitchen on summer evenings, before their band of growing children dispersed in all directions. I thought of Jim and Mary Whelan on the other side, their quiet ways and his giant figure smiling down on us as we passed from one yard to the next. And, one by one, the neighbours came alive.

Pat Behan, who could be counted on to get the oldest of cars going, even on the frostiest of winter mornings. And Dinah Whelan, who rang the angelus bell at twelve and six. And Nellie and Dick Thorpe in whose garden I'd swear I once saw a falling star crash to earth, though I could never find it afterwards. And over the next fence but one was Mrs O'Rourke who made the best mashed potato and milk I've ever tasted; and the Kinsellas – Mammy K and her daughters who were my childhood nannies and my confidantes when trouble came; and Harry Kinsella, who traipsed tiredly up the road each night, his long day's farm labouring done. And there were Paddy and Mariah Byrne; and Tom and Mrs Byrne; and O'Connells and Corrigans and Lawlers and Betty and the Barber Byrne – all these ghost figures, alive and dead, cycling home from work; pushing prams; tilling long gardens; pruning old roses; exchanging freshly cut flowers and newly dug potatoes across the wire fences; sharing the produce earned by the sweat of their brows. And there they were, in harder times, sending reticent children ducking and diving between the wire ribbons in search of *the lend of a cup of sugar* or a pound of butter or a jug of milk *just until tomorrow, mind.*

And, yes, there were tragedies – the youngster caught beneath the wheel of a coal lorry on a winter evening; the pregnancies that sent young women away to God alone knew where; the early deaths of men who were worked too hard but, through it all, we children passed from a yard of weeping relatives to the sanctuary of someone else's joy; from the threat of what we probably deserved to the hideouts beneath tall rhubarb leaves. There was always somewhere to go and somewhere to rest and open back doors and, when all else failed, a cut of bread and jam or a place beside a blazing range or a hand of cards on a winter night or a well-worn comic to pore over until a voice came calling from the yard next door, saying *Bed* or *Time for the rosary* or *Your sister says you're wanted.*

And then we'd climb slowly, theatrically between the loose wires, trudging slowly home, loathe to see the evening end but with that childhood certainty that tomorrow we could, again, slip easily from yard to yard and garden to garden in search of whatever innocence the world might offer to our senses.

Meadows and Byrnes

It was a radio advertisement that got me thinking and, once I started thinking, I knew I'd have to go back – so back I went, to look at a field in which we played as children. It's a long, broad field, sweeping from the road towards the river and it dips suddenly in the middle, taking an ice-age step down to the lower level and then tumbling gently into the slow waters of the river Lerr.

In my childhood we called the section that skirted the river *the Low Meadow* and the part that arched its back against the horizon was *the High Meadow*. The meadows were all one field but, when you're eight years old, one end of a field is as far from the other as childhood is from middle age. It was the place in which we got lost on summer days; the outlaws hiding place; the wastes of Arizona; the deep forests of Africa, and the trenches of the Somme.

But the *Low* and *High Meadows* weren't the only ones in our parish – the countryside was dotted with them, beautiful fields of deep, rich grass into which we could plunge with delight, our bicycles abandoned at the gates, six children dismounting in chaos from two cycles – one on the saddle, one on the carrier and one on the bar of each battered pushbike. The meadows were sweet and warm, their grasses spattered with flowers – poppies and buttercups and dandelions and primroses and cowslips and yard-tall daisies. The fields drew us in like enormous paintings. And there were meadows on every road – Joe Clinton's on Crop Hill; Brown's in Woodlands; Dempsey's on Barn Hill; Wright's and Nolan's and Wall's and Greene's and O'Gorman's. It seemed as though there were an eternity of meadows, each one wider, deeper, warmer than the last.

But now, as I discovered on my visit, virtually every field is tilled. The High and Low Meadows are already alive with slim, green lances of corn. The headlands hold a clump or two of primroses, but the cowslips have retreated to the railway embankments at Maganey. The endless meadows of childhood have disappeared behind the locked and bolted farm gates that replaced the metal sunrise pattern of the gates I knew in childhood. But that plethora of missing meadows was only half the story. The other half, also inspired by the radio advertisement, got me thinking, in turn, about the abundance of Byrnes in the village of my youth.

There was the Priest's Paddy, who lived at Carlow Gate and worked as a gardener for the Parish Priest; there was Pat the Barber, who put a short plank across the arms of his barber's chair to raise us little fellows up and make life easier for him when he cut our hair on Saturday afternoons. There was Paddy who sat beside me in school and duetted with me on *The Pub with no Beer* in third class. There was Red Paddy – so called for his hair, not his politics. There was Paddy the shop, who lived at the end of our terrace but ran a shop across the road from the Castle Cinema. The cinema had no sweet shop so, at half-time, between the little picture and the big picture, we'd pour out of the cinema, cross the street and pick up a quarter pound of Lemon and Lime sweets or an ice-cream, when it was in stock. Those were the days when ice-cream was seasonal – May to September.

Not that all the male Byrnes in Castledermot were called Paddy. There was Locky and Billy and Jimmy and Hugh who worked in the Shamrock Bar – as kids we'd call in on hot summer afternoons and ask for a glass of water, knowing he'd top the water up with lime cordial. There were the village Byrnes and the country Byrnes. There were Byrnes in Ballyhade and Byrnes at Carlow Gate. There was Betty the hairdresser and Mrs Byrne who had a cure for the *maoinearach*, a version of ME that seemed only to occur in the Barrow valley. There were Byrnes who farmed and Byrnes who worked on farms. There was Tom, there was Pat, there was Ger, there was the Sport and there was the Baw. There was Noel who was born on Christmas Eve, and, years later, in my teaching days, there were Byrnes who came on the school bus and Byrnes who walked and Byrnes who cycled in from the country. There were Byrnes who sang and Byrnes who played football; Byrnes who starred on the basketball court and Byrnes who were nuns and priests...the list went on and on.

And the wonderful thing is – even though the meadows are going or gone – the Byrnes are as prolific as they ever were. Long may they be so.

Mowing the Lawn

It's been one of those years when the grass just goes on growing and the strawberries and apple trees are putting out their flowers again. One of those Indian summers and it reminds me of another summer many moons ago and grass that kept on growing.

It was September 1969. It was a Saturday afternoon and I was sixteen years old and I had a lot of things to do – music to hear; books to read; teenage poetry to write; romantic imaginings to pursue; friends to meet. Were there enough hours in the day, I wondered, to get all these things done? And there was a disco to prepare for, a weekend hop in the youth club that night. I was busy, busy, busy so, when my mother informed me that the lawn needed cutting and that I'd better get it done before the rain came and that she and my father were heading to Tullamore to see my aunt and wouldn't be back until late that night, my shoulders sagged, the long sigh came, my eyes lifted to the heavens and I let her know that I really wasn't impressed with this intrusion into my hectic teenage life. It was all about body language before I had any idea what body language was.

"And you needn't have that *attitude*," my mother said. "It'll take you twenty minutes. Just get it done." My mother was Principal in the local Girls' National School and every so often, whenever we had an *attitude*, she'd go into Principal mode – the tone of her voice would deepen; the pace of delivery would slow and the face would grow stern. We knew then that it was time to pack up the attitude and get on with the work.

Time slid by like a child on an icy road and, before I knew it, the angelus bell was ringing. Taking the lawnmower from the shed, I wheeled it around to the lawn. I just want to remind you that we're talking 1969 here

– no ride-on or petrol-driven mowers this was a run of the mill hand-push mower; you push the mower, the blades turn. You stop, they stop.

The lawn that lay before me wasn't particularly big – thirty feet by twenty perhaps – but I'd always been bored by the notion of cutting up and down and up and down, line on line, till the grass was laid low. I much preferred making unusual patterns, cutting the grass in sections until suddenly there was nothing left to cut.

That Saturday afternoon, my parents safely stowed in Tullamore, and still being annoyed that the job had fallen to me, I thought I'd be a little adventurous and, lifting the mower into the middle of the lawn I mowed a very large letter A through the grass. It was about eight feet tall and it stood out from the longer, daisy-dotted grass about it. Lifting the mower to the right, I then mowed a matching R. My mood lightened. This was fun. A lift to the right and a large and careful S was mown. And, finally, one more lift to the right and an eight-foot E was added.

Climbing onto the garden wall, I viewed my handiwork from on high. It was clear to see and clear to read and it summed up my attitude to the work that had been inflicted on me. And then, like the Red Sea parting for Moses, the clouds above were torn asunder and rain flapped down in driving sheets. I ran for the shelter of the shed and waited and waited and waited for the torrent to end. And end it did. Twenty minutes later.

Let me say here that the hand-push mower is a wonderful implement and when Edwin Beard Budding invented it in 1830, he eased a lot of lives. What he didn't crack, however, was the problem I faced on that evening in August 1969. When grass is long and wet, the push mower will not cut it. Try as I might, shove and grunt and swear and sweat, the blades would turn, then clog in the wet grass – there was no progress to be made. My handiwork was semi-permanently installed for all to see.

By nine, when I headed for the youth club disco, darkness was falling. I knew my parents wouldn't see the result of my labour in the dark of night and I planned on getting up early on the Sunday morning and finishing the job before they had a chance to read my message. And, conscientious as I was, I set my alarm that night, determined to get the job finished at six a.m. And I did wake and I did leave my bed and I did creep downstairs – to be faced with a deluge of rain.

My *grassito* went unnoticed until half past ten that morning. As my father backed the car out of the garage for Mass, my mother closed the front door and turned to meet him at the gate.

"You didn't get the lawn finished," she said.

"No, the rain came. But I will... later."

We walked down the concrete path and my mother sat into the car beside my father. I scrambled into the rear seat. Only as we backed down the short driveway did my handiwork become clear, the letters seeming to stretch forever across the grass. The A, the R, the S and the E, there for all – especially my mother – to see. I watched her shoulders tighten, heard the quiet sigh, knew exactly what she was thinking – about the neighbours and passers-by on their way to Mass and her pupils and their parents and self-respect and why could I not, just this once, have done what I'd been asked and have a modicum of common sense instead of *that attitude* and look where it had got us now... I waited, knowing the thoughts would presently be articulated and in no uncertain terms.

Oh and, of course, it rained and rained till the following Tuesday afternoon.

Halcyon Days

I was listening to Gladys Knight's version of 'The Way We Were' recently, you know the one that begins, with the spoken word: *Hey, you know everybody's talking about the good old days right? Everybody. The good old days, the good old days. Well let's talk about the good old days...*

A week later I was looking at some photographs someone had posted on the Castledermot Historical Society Facebook page. There were notes underneath, memories of happy childhood times, comments about the red hayshed on Main Street, the one where Paddy Hickey smoked borrowed Woodbines, the one where we sheltered from the rain, the one that no one seemed to own – was it Doyle's? Was it Nolan's? Was it the County Council's? It didn't matter much to us – it was a shelter from the rain and the pain of poverty, a place to loiter on our way from school, a safe haven for smokers and – rumour had it – a place for the shenanigans that followed dances. Not that we knew anything about dances back then and shenanigans couldn't even be imagined.

A couple of days after that a friend remarked on the fact that five cherry trees had been broken by vandals on the Square in the town where he now lives and how *it would never have happened when we were kids, never, that kind of thing just wouldn't be allowed.*

And then, out of somewhere, came the memory of an incident I had almost forgotten. An incident from the halcyon days of childhood, that time when, as memory fools us into believing, the summers were sunny and the days were long and everyone was happy and all was well with the world.

It's 1958 and at the end of our road there's a grass triangle where we children gather in the evenings. It's just on the bend where the road turns

105

for the village and it backs onto the field that divides our cul-de-sac from the church grounds. And, on this summer evening, I wander aimlessly down the road in search of something called adventure. Joe Whelan is standing on the path at the end of the road, a mat of burnt, sodden fur on the grass triangle across from him.

A man comes from one of the houses near the triangle, carrying a sack and a shovel. He lifts the fur and we see legs dangling over the side of the shovel. What might be a head lolls on the handle. The man holds the sack open and slides the burned carcass inside. He scrapes the ground where the unfortunate animal had lain down to die.

"What happened?"

"Someone set fire to a dog," Joe says. "Some of the boys from the town. They tied a can to his tail and set him on fire at Carlow Gate and ran him down here."

"Did you see it?"

"No. Mr Byrne told me. He threw a bucket of water over him but he was nearly dead by then."

We watch the man carry the sack across his garden and lay it gently on the grass. He starts to dig a hole.

"Whose dog was it?"

"Don't know. A stray, I think."

The sun is beginning to fall as we walk back up the road; the sound of digging follows us. And then we get on with doing something else, we get on with our lives, we change direction in search of another adventure and, because we need to or because we can, we allow the memory to fade.

What is it Gladys Knight says then? Come to think of it, as bad as they are, these will come to be the good old days for our children.

Everything changes and nothing changes and we're all susceptible to that condition called human.

The Leather Football

When my brother was a young boy, he cycled the fourteen-mile round trip, to and from Carlow, to secondary school. He was a small boy on a big bicycle, wind and rain; twilight and dusk; September to June. That would have been our mother's idea. Get a good education. Education was everything, the teacher in her said. And our father would have agreed. He'd left school early to work on the railways, like his father, like his brother. And he regretted his lack of schooling. Not that he often said it but he said it now and again and he said it all the time when it came to our education.

That was the mid-nineteen fifties. We were still living on the Low Terrace, still four years away from moving to the High Terrace with its bathroom and its sitting-room and its three upstairs bedrooms. So every morning my brother and a few other boys would head out of Castledermot, up the long push from the village, then downhill past Wright's farm and on through Knocknagee and into Carlow to the Christian Brothers' School. I knew nothing about this. I was the bow-legged two-year old on the swing, falling when I walked, walking when I didn't.

But that journey wasn't just about school. There were piano lessons thrown in on Saturday afternoons, when my brother had finished his half-day of schooling. He got the better of our mother on that one, though, and spent those afternoons in the cinema, using the piano-lesson money to get him there.

Years afterwards, as a teenager myself, I couldn't but admire his coolness in carrying that off. I couldn't have. But by the time I got to hear the story, the storm had blown over and it was just another laughable legend. *Do you remember the time…*

108

When we brought my brother's ashes home from America, fifty-one years after the dodged piano lessons, there were hundreds of people in the church for the funeral mass. Most of them with stories about him – from medical days; college days; boarding school days; those days when he cycled to Carlow. And there were stories of that summer when he'd finished first year and worked as a beet thinner.

For some reason I was never allowed to thin beet. I asked, every summer from fifth-class onwards, if I could thin beet and every year I was turned down at home. Stephen Spender wasn't the only one whose parents kept him from children who were rough.

After my brother's burial, a man came to me in the cemetery and talked about the days when they had played football together.

"He was a poor footballer but he had the leather ball, so he was always included," he said.

I listened and nodded and smiled but, all the time, I was thinking of the truer, darker story.

It was the summer of 1956. My brother was fourteen. He wanted to save enough money to buy a leather football and thinning beet was one way to do it. Hard work in dry, hot weather or cool wet weather – one as bad as the other – but lots of farmers looking for people to do the work, hours on your knees, back bent, row by row across the long, rough, pebbled ground. Ironically, the hurling and football finals were postponed that year owing to an outbreak of polio. And that was the last summer for 42 years in which our native Kildare would win a Leinster senior football championship. Caught up in the euphoria of the time, my brother wanted that new football and he was prepared to work for it.

And that's what he did – worked hard, saved his money and, eventually, bought the leather ball. There were matches with his friends, in the football field behind our house, matches that stretched endlessly across summer afternoons until the fall of night called the players home. And most nights my brother left the ball in the garden, ready for the following morning's play, there among the summer toys and the car tyres that were our horses.

And then, one sunny morning, he came out of the house to find that someone had taken a penknife to the ball and stabbed it until it was punctured beyond repair. An act of stupid destruction, two fingers to everything my brother had worked for.

He knew the culprit had to be someone who was familiar with him. There were less than 700 people living in the village at the time but only a dozen or so would have known that he had the ball.

And so, half a century later, I stood in the cemetery, listening to this man who had no idea of the murky story behind his own fond memories, and I glanced at the flowers piled on my brother's grave and wondered if he ever quite got over that wanton act of betrayal, and it made my sadness all the deeper because I knew he loved this village every bit as much as I did. And I hoped his dying memories had been of happier days: of films caught on the mitch from piano lessons; of the laughter of young boys freewheeling home from beet-thinning on a hot summer afternoon; of a football soaring high on a late and golden evening long ago before the world turned darker.

After My Brother Died

I gave my soul to loneliness; I gave my body to fear; I went to dark places from which I've never quite come back; I longed for a warm, slow stroll with him, across the evening beach;

I longed for one last long late-night conversation; I tried to dream but the dreams refused to run; I wore his shirt; I went to where his ashes lie and I listened but no one spoke;

I was desolate; I doubted everything but most of all I doubted myself; I woke up suspecting the truth; I went on living day to day; I worked; I laughed and then resented my laughter; I tried to pray but my prayers were a paper in the wind; I drove past the old house and stared at the empty window of the room that had been ours; I tried to understand; I decorated the Christmas tree; I threatened my son on Christmas Day and afterwards I hugged him;

I lost my mind but the loss was not so great; I wanted to believe; I wanted my brother's faith, his hope, his great belief in the things that we'd been taught; I wanted him to be, just that, simply to have him here; I walked each day through hedges of quince; I was fearful and then I was afraid of my fear; I was afraid; I wanted never to forget; I longed for forgetfulness; I kept his email address on my computer; I kept his phone number in my book; I framed his photograph and photographs of the two of us together; I played the music he loved; I walked and walked, as though he might be waiting in the forest; I watched my dog for signs of some sixth sense; I lost the place that divides need and want; I cried; I was afraid of how we grow to be the very thing we fear.

Climbing Mount Eros

They say mountains teach you things.

Climbing in the dawning light was the easy part. The breeze was strong and it kept the heat at bay. By the time we were half-way up Mount Eros, the sun was edging over the horizon and the temperature beginning to muscle up into the high twenties. But then I thought of Croagh Patrick and it made the zig-zag climb up this Greek mountain seem like a stroll in the park.

At the summit, to our disappointment, we found that the bell we had rung three years previously was no longer there, though the view was every bit as stunning, the Saronic islands and Saronikos Bay below us, and the empty, blue sky stretching away like an untouched canvas above. The wind in our ears rose and fell, like the early morning argument of the Gods.

The sun went on rising, as is its wont, the soaring temperatures and the suddenly fading wind reminding us, however, that mountain tops are for reaching and leaving, they're not places to stay. And so began the descent. The shale which had remained steady underfoot on our ascent seemed anxious not to provide a firm foothold on the way down; the rocks, which had been anchors to hoist us on the way up, became encumbrances to be overcome or circumnavigated as we descended. The scrawny bushes that had provided a little shade on the climb seemed suddenly to have grown with no greater purpose than to block our way.

At one point, I found myself sliding down on my backside, a carpet of moving shale beneath me, my destination in the hands of the mountain gullies. And then, out of nowhere, a memory came back to me of the four-year-old boy who was me; the boy who climbed the church stairs of the

112

main gallery in Castledermot church with his family every Sunday morning for 11 o'clock Mass; the same boy who baulked at the sight of those stairs when Mass had ended; the stubborn child who refused to be carried by his father but insisted, instead, on descending, one step at a time, on his backside while the crowds behind, anxious to get to Mary Nolan's or George Abbot's shops for the Sunday paper, anxious to get to football matches or Sunday lunches waited, impatiently for me to complete my slow descent.

With the ending of my uncontrolled shale train on a patch of red clay on the side of Eros, the childhood memory evaporated and I was faced with rocks over which I clambered awkwardly. In those moments, I wished for the suppleness of youth, for the return of the body that had never opened a gate or gone around a wall; the legs that climbed or cleared those walls and gates; the body that would have scampered easily across these sunburnt boulders and gone in search of bigger.

And then, as I stopped to catch my breath and down a gulp of water I saw in that 64-year-old man on the side of that burning mountain an individual who was blessed and fortunate beyond belief. I glimpsed the monastery below me with its shaded courtyard and its cold, well-drawn water; with its container of loukoumi, sweet and refreshing and free to the passing traveller. I sensed my constant companion at my shoulder, making her way over a boulder twice the size of the one in my path, her sunlit dress the colour, I imagined, of an angel's tunic. And I thought of the pleasure of that morning's climb and the warm scent of the twisting path that runs through pine woods on the lower levels of the mountain. I thought of life, of the things we call life, the things we live through – the mistakes we make, the joys we find, the goodness we try to do; the moments when we fall and the moments when we rise and I was grateful to be on that mountain with the hot sunlight on my head; grateful to be able to make that descent; grateful for the water and the sweets and the shadow and the sunlight that lay below me. Glad, above all, to be alive.

Even small mountains teach big lessons.

Hart Island, New York

The poor are always with us,

expecting a fair deal, a square meal,

depending on what's given, hunting for a box to live in.

The poor are always with us,

hoping against hope, clinging to a fraying rope,

knowing life is fucking hard, never turning the trump card.

The poor are always with us,

no intensive care, just undiagnosed despair,

their land of the free is a trench in Potter's Field.

The poor are always with us,

an industrial grave for the hopeless and the brave

and afterwards the silence. Each one an island.

The poor are always with us at the midnight hour,

a despondent congregation in the shadow of the Tower.

Unbelievable Holiday Snaps

Is it just me or have you ever noticed that well of unbridled enthusiasm that springs up every time you ask someone about a holiday destination you're considering, one they have already visited? And have you ever noticed that the more remote the destination, the more eager people are to tell you about it and about why it's the only – *and I mean only* – place you should ever consider holidaying. Not alone that but *you simply must, must, must go there*. And with this they flick open their i-phones and treat you to forty-seven views of the self-same place.

But, better still, they go on to regale you with a long and detailed story about the wonderful – nay the fantastic, the *OMG experience* they had there.

The story usually begins with the *unbelievable* apartment they found, by chance of course, courtesy of a man standing under a lamppost on a corner outside a wonderful bistro. The apartment always overlooks the sea and, naturally, there are views of distant mountains and the perpetual lapping of waves on a golden beach – but not just any beach. This one is five miles long and a mile wide and there's never anyone else on it or, if there is, he's a tanned and hunky lifeguard who speaks nine languages fluently and in a voice that is as close to mahogany as a voice can come – a cross between Leonard Cohen and Tom Waits but sixty years younger than either – oh and he plays Spanish guitar when he's not preparing for a marathon.

And then the tale includes, as it always does, a trip to a remote restaurant where the owner and his wife are so extraordinarily welcoming that they treat the visitors like long-lost cousins, once they discover they're Irish and not English. Not only do they put up a meal fit for a king and queen but the owners' son plays the balalaika and their daughter sings regional songs that make "Danny Boy" sound like something from the Bay City Rollers. And, to cap it all, the meal – five expansive courses – comes to less than €30 and that includes three bottles of *a really precocious little local wine.*

But, as your friends will tell you gleefully, warming to the tale, it doesn't end there. The local taxi-driver, a complete shyster it turns out, doesn't turn up to collect them at the appointed time, having been commandeered by a bunch of boozy English/American/German tourists – delete as appropriate. So the restaurateur and his wife insist they stay for the night, turfing their children out to sleep in barrels on the terrace behind the restaurant in order to give them a decent room.

Then, in the morning, nothing will do the restaurant owner but to serve up a full breakfast before the guests leave. But the story doesn't end there – not on your life. This is the moment where the tale reaches its zenith, the moment where the donkeys appear. There's always a donkey or two in these stories and there will be half-a-dozen photographs to accompany this section of the narrative.

The restaurant owners' son will saddle two donkeys and his parents will insist on putting two carafes of the aforementioned precocious little wine in the saddlebags, along with some smoked local ham, that morning's bread and a necklace for luck. And then the son will lead the donkeys and their precious riders down a steep mountain trail – with further photographs to accompany this part of the journey, too – and deposit them safely at their hotel door. There, against his will, my friends will force twenty euro into the young donkey-driver's reluctant fist and thank him for his kindness.

And there the tale might finally end – but no.

"Do you know what it is?" one of them asks.

I shake my head.

"Six weeks after we got back, didn't this parcel arrive from the couple in the restaurant and in it was a bolt of local silk. They said the young fellow should never have taken the money from us and this was their way of saying thanks. They got our address from the hotel."

"Amazing," I say.

"I'd show it to you but I had a dress made up from it for my sister for her fiftieth."

I nod.

"But I'll tell you one thing, if you're heading there on holiday you really have to visit the Cehennem restaurant and ask for Ahmed. And be sure to tell him we sent you."

John Clare

On the afternoon of 20 May 1864, just before three in the afternoon, the English poet John Clare drew his last breath in Northampton Asylum. "He simply ceased to breathe" the official report said. And so a tortured but beautiful life drew to a close. The peasant poet had died within the walls of the hospital that had been his home for decades.

Clare was born in Helpston, near Peterborough, in July 1793, the son of a farm labouring, wrestling father and a mother who had ambitions for her book-loving son. Not that ambitions paid bills or put food on a table. John followed his father into the world of farm labouring and, when work was scarce in the fields, into lime-burning, gardening and any other handiwork he could find. But his aspirations lay elsewhere.

From early boyhood he had a love of wild places and wild things and a love of writing. Even in his school days he read what he could and wrote where he could – on scraps of paper, on bags, on the blank pages of books and in the notebooks he bought with the pennies he could save.

But writing was not the only driving force in the young man's life. There was love, too. First for Mary Joyce, a schoolmate and the daughter of a farmer. The class structure in rural England ensured that the relationship would never work, though Clare never forgot Mary. Patty Turner became his wife, after she discovered she was pregnant, and she it was who stood by him in bad times and good.

The good days were the ones where his poetry was published; where patrons supplied the family with a new house and food and possibilities. The bad days were the ones where John's epilepsy, drinking and mental health problems led him into troubled times.

And then there was his opposition to the enclosure of lands that had been commonage for centuries. His willingness to speak out against the land-grabbing of the gentry lost him many prospective supporters among the wealthy landowners and his opposition to hunting and badger-baiting lost him friends among his own class – the peasants of Northampton.

Ill-health, poverty and the confusion and frustration of being at one moment the darling of the monied classes, paraded around London, and at the next being returned to his life of field work and hardship broke Clare's mental and physical health and he was committed to High Beech Asylum in Essex in 1737. But Essex was not Northampton and, four years later, Clare escaped from the liberal institution and set off walking for home – a journey he recorded in his writings. Not only did he want to get home, he wanted to be reunited with the woman he described as his "first wife" – his schoolmate Mary Joyce, who was already dead, the victim of a house fire.

Initially, his family welcomed the poet home, but his health and behaviour deteriorated and, just after Christmas1841, he was committed to Northampton Asylum – an institution in which he would spend the next twenty-three years, believing at times that he was Lord Byron or the Captain of a ship or a well-known wrestler and believing always that Mary Joyce and he would be reunited.

Northampton Asylum was, again, a reasonably liberal hospital and Clare was well cared for and was free to come and go in the gardens surrounding the building. He was free, too, to write and this he continued to do – between the debilitating bouts of epilepsy and insanity. When these struck he claimed "they have cut the top off my head and removed all the vowels so that I cannot write".

And yet the poems came – sometimes ballads and songs and sometimes deeper, darker works, like his poem, *I Am*, a life story in a sonnet:

I am: yet what I am none cares or knows,

My friends forsake me like a memory lost;

I am the self-consumer of my woes,

They rise and vanish in oblivions host,

Like shadows in love's frenzied stifled throes

And yet I am! and live with vapours tost

Into the nothingness of scorn and noise,

Into the living sea of waking dreams,

Where there is neither sense of life or joys,

But the vast shipwreck of my life's esteems;

Even the dearest—that I loved the best—

Are strange—nay, rather, stranger than the rest.

I long for scenes where man hath never trod;

A place where woman never smil'd or wept;

There to abide with my creator, God,

And sleep as I in childhood sweetly slept:

Untroubling and untroubled where I lie;

The grass below—above the vaulted sky.

And then, on 20 May 1864 he died. His body was taken back to Helpston and buried there. Untroubling and untroubled, he lies in the village graveyard, home at last, the grass below – above the vaulted sky.

Bogwoman

One time, a long way from home
and from the things that were familiar,
she saw an African woman at a bus stop
on the King's Road. It was summertime.

The woman's skin reminded her
of how the evening sky dilutes in bog pools,
letting its colours linger with the promise
of long days still to come. And she

walked up to the silent, motionless woman
and touched the side of her shining face
and the woman smiled and held her hand
for an enduring moment. Two souls at sea,

each far from a homeland and from a time
when life was more than simply memory.

The Lane

I've walked this lane virtually every day for the last five years. I stumbled on it, almost by accident, when a flood closed the river path I would normally take. I have never been totally enamoured by the river walk, there's something about its flow in winter, the darkness and speed of the water, that speaks of threat and destruction. Perhaps my reticence stems from the fact that I'm not a good swimmer and any accidental struggle between me and the river could have only one outcome.

So, with the river bank flooded, I needed to find a new pathway for my dog and myself and there was the lane, curving beneath hundred-year-old trees; skirting fields where cattle and sheep grazed and crops sprouted and grew and were harvested. At first, it was simply a place to walk, a laneway on which there was little traffic, a road that at two points offered divergent paths – not in a yellow wood but in sight of Mount Leinster and the Blackstairs Mountains. Those early winter walks were often taken, head down, in the teeth of a gale or the icy sting of falling sleet but, as that first spring came on, the lane revealed itself as a place with a living history.

Banks of primroses suddenly lit up the morning gloom of March; clumps of daffodils, apparently growing wild, bounded the remnant of a long forgotten garden and, as it revealed itself to me, that, in turn, led to the almost-disappeared relic of a cottage and the bare outline of a home that housed a family a century ago. A bank of celandine lit what would, once, have been a back garden. A fallen tree revealed a hedge of wild lilac surging in waves of scent and colour on a warm May breeze. Bluebells suddenly appeared in the shadow of a small stand of trees and wild apples budded and bloomed and leaned low to offer their fruit in autumn.

By the end of my first year of walking the lane, I had seen it in all its colours and it had begun to reveal its histories. But it took another two years before my own investigations, and the occasional conversation with people I met on my rambles, started the process of piecing together the stories of the people who been born and lived and died in the cottages which were now long gone.

On closer inspection, a crumbling wall revealed the outlines of the doorways and windows of half a dozen cottages. A cul-de-sac, that offered a raging flame of ripening blackberries in late summer and a feast of fruit in early autumn, disclosed a crumbling farmhouse when winter stripped the entangled branches of the bramble. I spent an hour wandering through the empty, roofless rooms while my dog nosed about the headland of the field behind. The ghost-voices of generations of a family seemed to whisper their urgent stories in my ear but each story was lifted and taken by the wind, leaving only my imagination to recreate the lives and loves and losses of the people who had come and gone through this now doorless doorway.

Across from the ruined house, a scatter of forget-me-nots spoke their own silent reminder of the past and it struck me, as I stood in that doorway, that the sun that shone piecemeal through the patchwork of bare branches on the other side of the lane was the same sun that had shone on the women and men who had stood beneath this now sagging lintel a hundred and fifty years ago. And they, too, must have wondered at the beauty of the world and the turning of one season into another. Wondered at the way the world goes on in spite, rather than because, of us.

So, year by year, this lane has slowly offered me its stories and its beauty, its sheltered spots in winter deluges and its stunning views of mountain and river in spring and summer.

Just last week, I stood on a headland above the waters of the Barrow chatting with Joe Somers, who lives in the last house on the lane. He pointed to a hedgerow at the other end a field.

"That was where the old Mass path ran," he said. "It led down to the river." And he pointed to the derelict remains of a bridge across the Barrow. "People would take it as a short cut from Leighlinbridge to Bagenalstown for Mass."

In that moment another piece of history was revealed and another choir of voices murmured that their stories, too, deserved to be heard. The landscape holds those stories as, in time, it will hold ours.

Meeting Pete Seeger

It was a bright summer morning and the train out of New York's Grand Central station was headed the sixty miles or so North for Beacon and in the seventy-five minutes it took to get there I had plenty of time to wonder about the man I was on my way to visit. I knew a lot about him and even more about his music; he was godfather by proxy to my son and we'd communicated by letter over the years, yet we'd never met.

Beacon isn't a big town but it was even smaller in the 1990's – with a population of less than 15,000 people. The railway station reminded me of Limerick Junction – with better weather. Three tracks, a basic platform and very few people alighting in the warm morning air. But there, at the other end of that platform, was the man I'd come to meet – tall and gangly, bearded and smiling – Pete Seeger.

We shook hands and he led me to the battered pick-up parked outside and we drove the winding road that became a winding track to his home in the woods above the Hudson River. And there we spent the day, talking about music ... politics and poetry. We rambled in the forest that surrounded the house he'd built himself and the house that replaced it. We sat in the sun and he played his guitar and sang some songs and we talked about the Spanish Civil War and he broke into song again, songs from the Spanish trenches.

"I almost forgot, we haven't eaten," he said and while I answered his questions about Ireland and the state of the nation and the poets I admired and where I thought the politics north and south of the border might lead us, he made a salad, produced some bread and coffee and invited me to sit and eat, and all without drawing breath.

126

The interesting thing for me was that in the previous week I'd interviewed two songwriters in New York city and, in each case, the ego was the thing I remembered most. But here was a man who had played with Woody Guthrie; a man blacklisted for his politics; a man whose songs had been known and sung and still are known and sung and loved around the world – songs like *If I had a Hammer; Turn, Turn, Turn; Oh, Had I a Golden Thread* and *Where Have All the Flowers Gone* – and the only ego in sight was his blazing commitment to music and justice and laughter and equality and the environment and the huddled masses, whether they were sixty miles down the line in New York or on the streets of Cambodia or Vietnam or of South America.

Meeting a hero is a tricky business – we travel with our own expectations and, often, our own delusions but we also travel in the hope that the people we've admired will be more or less the people we meet. With Pete Seeger the expectations were fulfilled and more.

In the afternoon, he showed me his daughter's kiln and some of her pottery; we inspected the woodpile, chopped and stacked by himself and he gave me all the information I'd ever need on the best timbers for burning and how they should be rotated, and then he produced a tin whistle from the pocket of his jeans and played me some tunes before taking me back inside to make more coffee.

Before I packed up my bits and pieces and prepared to leave, I asked if he'd sing me one last song – one of my favourites – *Rainbow Race*. And he did, sitting at his sunlit table, the woods above us; the Hudson below us. I closed my eyes and listened to the words that ring with truth about the blue sky above us and the one, round, green earth.

Afterwards, he drove me back to Beacon railway station and insisted on waiting with me on the platform till the New York bound train arrived. In the evening sun, on the speeding train, I closed my eyes and heard the words and the voice and the philosophy that have made Pete Seeger the man he is.

To Everything There Is a Season

There's a bend in the road, one point nine kilometres from home. I've named it Covid Corner. When I get to that point on my evening rambles, I cross the road and head back the way I've come.

These rambles have been blessed by good weather and the field on one side is ablaze with the yellow flame of rapeseed; on the other, the long field is dotted with sheep and lambs and a broken hedge of ancient thorns that runs down to the river, the remnant of another time when fields were smaller and life was even harder than it is now.

Whether it's the lambs or the sheep or the ancient ditch, I find my mind being drawn, on these twilit meanderings, to questions biblical. I have begun composing replies from the Romans and Thessalonians and Corinthians to Paul's letters and tirades. I imagine groups of men and women sitting around fires, discussing the correct wording of their responses. I hear voices raised in anger: a man suggests telling Paul where to get off; the quieter voice of a woman urges caution; there's a suggestion that they deny ever receiving his missives and blame it on the unreliable postal system of the time.

But last night something in the air took me back even further, to the book of Ecclesiastes and I began to wonder about the man or woman who composed that volume. And then I thought about the beautiful third chapter that begins: *To everything there is a season...* and I found myself speculating on what the author might have made of the current situation. I imagined the writer confined to home, a forty-something-year-old with a spouse and two children, both in their teens. And, just for the heck of it, I gave the family a pet terrapin.

129

With that, I handed the puzzled writer a blank sheet of paper and a pen and allowed them the freedom of my sometimes bizarre imagination. And this was the outcome:

To everything there is a season and a time to every tortoise under heaven. A time to get up in the morning, because it's good to stick to a routine, and a time to turn off Netflix at night; a time to plant the seven packets of seeds you bought online and a time to dig out the beetroot that has grown all winter and will never be cooked or eaten; a time to kill the neighbours, two doors down, who play heavy-metal in the garden late into the evening and a time to try to heal that rift with the neighbour who jumped the queue at the car wash when such things mattered; a time to break down the wall of the kids' bedroom and get them out into the air and a time to build up some brownie points with the in-laws; a time to weep for the fact that the Tiger King series was padded beyond endurance and a time to smirk, but sadly, at the thought that many of its participants will vote in the next U.S. Presidential election; a time to mourn the fact that there won't be a football kicked in anger all summer and Dublin will, thus, remain unbeaten and a time to dance to the sound of the Killers Human because it seems to catch the state of the race; a time to cast away stones that harbour slugs in the raised bed and a time to gather stones together for flinging at the neighbours, two doors down, who are still playing that bloody heavy metal; a time to remember embracing, because it has become a thing of the past, and a time to refrain from embracing long-lost friends in the supermarket car park because that's what the yellow leaflet says; a time to get online to order that book that you've been meaning to read since you were eighteen and a time to lose all patience with the internet that keeps slipping offline because of the faulty cable at the end of the street; a time to keep quiet about the terrapin's cage not being cleaned and a time to clear out the attic and cast away those football programmes which will never alter the fulltime score in ninety-eight; a time to rend that t-shirt that used to be loose on you, while doing the ad-break Jumping Jacks during Operation Transformation and a time to admit you only feel so/so; a time to keep your mouth shut and stay silent and a time to tell the kids what you really think of them and their terrapin; a time to love the world in all its natural beauty and a time to admit that you're beginning to hate the neighbours, two doors down, with their heavy metal dumpdumpdump; a time to plan a campaign of war against them that involves cutting down an electricity pole and a time of peace as you reach the 2K point on the road and stop to enjoy a silence that knows nothing of Metallica and Motorhead.

To everything there is, indeed, a season and brighter seasons will follow.

Autumn

The Arrival of Autumn

Recently I was part of a long discussion about the arrival of autumn. There were two of us involved – my constant companion and myself – and neither one was willing to give an inch on their strongly argued views – though my own stand was more to do with rising the companion than any deeply held belief.

"It definitely doesn't come until the school holidays are over," she said. "In fact, I'd go further and say that since the schools reopen now in August, autumn absolutely doesn't arrive until September and even then there's every chance of an Indian summer...which is still summer."

"Technically it arrives on August the first," I suggested only to be met with a barrage of suggestions that I was a killjoy and a pessimist and, worse still, that I was ignoring the fact "that Irish summers work to their own timetables."

"So what are the three months of summer?" I asked.

"May, June, July and August," I was told with a smirk that said – *put that in your mathematical pipe and smoke it!*

To be truthful, I've always thought of autumn as a moveable feast, its timing governed by the places we're at in our lives. As a boy in primary school the arrival of that nagging pain in my gut at the thought of returning to the same building as one particular teacher heralded the end of summer – and it usually began about ten days before the holiday actually ended, so perhaps the accusation of pessimism was well merited.

In secondary school summer ended with the opening of the school door and the sweet, sickly smell of the waxed corridor floors and the oiled desks in the classrooms, followed by the sight of shining blackboards – awaiting

134

the letters of the Greek alphabet and the French verbs that were Greeker than Greek to me.

But by the time college came around – with its very liberal and relaxed return to lectures in October – I judged the arrival of autumn by the rust appearing on our next-door neighbour's dahlias. Mrs O'Connell's garden was filled all summer with every kind of horticultural combination but when the dahlias bloomed, it was like the first trumpets sounding distantly for the last day and by the time the petals had begun to tarnish and turn the colour of field gates, it was time to begin packing again for the flatlands of Dublin.

And so it went – in my teaching days I reverted to the smell of floor polish and wood oil but, as I've grown older, there is one sight, one smell and one sound that forever whisper *autumn* in my ear. The sight is that of smoke coiling among apple trees at the end of someone's garden; the smell is the smell of burning leaves and clippings; the sound is the gentle crack of dry grass, lopped branches and the occasional swish of a rake or fork turning the contents of the bonfire, urging the flames to rise and devour not just the wood and grass and leaves but to devour, too, the last rays and days of summer.

One morning last week, on the banks of the Barrow, near Milford Bridge in Co Carlow, as I walked the dog in warm sunshine, I caught, out of the corner of my eye, a lick of flame between some trees in a cottage garden and then I heard the crackle of fallen branches like a burning bush, and within seconds I smelled the smell of autumn smoke and I knew the season was upon me, if not upon my companion, still arguing the case for an Irish solution to an Irish calendar.

All the Moons in Our Sky

It was there, on the mantelpiece in a friend's house, the memoriam card, propped against a candlestick, the face of the lost one smiling out from a photograph taken in better and happier times. Underneath were the name and the date and then something I had never before seen on a memoriam card – a line that read: *Died during a blue moon.*

How beautiful I thought, how beautiful to live and die beneath blue moons. And afterwards, when I went in search of the history of the phrase, I came across more information than I'd expected, about the one great moon that is so many moons in our sky.

I grew up, as most of us did, with the expression *Once in a blue moon* and I knew that a blue moon was an extra full moon in a season or a second full moon in a calendar month and I knew that, now and again, the moon can appear to have a blue tint. And, of course, I knew the song. What I didn't know, however, was that there are dozens of names, many more than I'd imagined, for the moon in our firmament. And, what's more, differing traditions have widely differing names for the changes wrought on it by the seasons.

The April moon, not surprisingly, is generally a moon of growth. In Celtic times it was the Growing Moon, while in mediaeval England it was the Seed Moon and for the American Colonists it was the Planter's Moon. Look, though, at the names that the nomadic Native Americans had and you find the Cherokee people call it the Flower Moon, while for the Dakota Sioux it was the Moon When Geese Return in Scattered Formation.

Similarly, the summer moons reflect the lives of those who named them. In Celtic times the moons of May, June and July were the Bright Moon, the

Moon of Horses and the Moon of Claiming. The latter is a reflection of the times when the young tribal men would claim the women they loved.

In mediaeval England the summer moons were the Hare, Dyan and Mead – dyan meaning a pair or a pinnacle – reflective of the mid-season pinnacle of summer. For the Cherokee tribe, however, the summer moons were Planting, Green Corn and Ripe Corn – practical names. But for their Choctaw brothers, the middle months were seen in the Panther Moon, Windy Moon and Crane Moon.

Autumn and winter seemed to bring more creativity to the naming of the lunar cycles. In China, October, November and December brought Kindly, White and Bitter Moons, while for the Celts these months brought Harvest, Dark and Cold Moons. And for the mediaeval English, the moons, intriguingly, were Blood, Snow and Oak.

One thing is common across the traditions – the need to name the moon and, in so doing, to recognise the power it held and holds not only over the seas but over the imaginations of the people who lived in its light.

I find it difficult to imagine anyone in these days of electricity and constant light bothering to name the moons that sail the skies, and I find it wonderful to have these names to ponder and to realise how close it brings me to the times and people who named them. These were people for whom September brought the Singing Moon – a period, perhaps, of rest and celebration, once the harvest had been gathered. People for whom December brought the Long Night Moon, casting its brightness into the darkest days of the year. And so it goes until, again, the year comes round and we watch the Celtic moon of April – the Growing Moon.

Long may it grow, long may we all and, when the time comes, may it come beneath a big blue moon.

The Sixty-Four Pagers

Comics. Not the stand-up variety. The real thing. *The Beano. The Dandy. The Victor. Bunty. Judy.* They were the small-change of my youth. Bartered, traded, swopped and circulated like water through a central heating system. They were the lights in the darkest winters, the promise at the end of the longest week and the escape from the high-security prison of early-'sixties Ireland.

But they weren't top-dollar. That accolade was reserved for the 64-pagers. The classic comics that remained in circulation in Castledermot long after they'd ceased publication in 1962.

The man behind the sixty-four-pagers was Albert Lewis Kanter – a man we'd never heard of; a man to whom we owed so much without ever knowing it. Kanter was the man who put the first Classic Comic on the news-stands in 1941 – an adaptation of Alexandre Dumas' *The Three Musketeers*. It was followed by sixty-four--page versions of *Ivanhoe* and *The Count of Monte Cristo*.

One of Kanter's aims was to introduce people like me to great literature. I never knew this – which was probably just as well. I couldn't imagine Joe Whelan, Olive Hunt, Seán Healy, Michael O'Neill and myself sitting on Rice's Hill discussing the literary merits and the success or otherwise of Kanter's adaptations. What we did do was swap our comics – *The Beano*, *The Dandy* and *The Victor* were, at best, part of a three for one when it came to the bartering for 64-pagers.

There was something about the format that made the Classics just that – memorable, classy, seriously good. And it wasn't just the extra pages. It was the sense that you were getting something special with the 64-pager. A good story, a yarn that could be read at one sitting or several but one that detoured down alleyways. We had no idea what subplot or character development meant but we knew a good read when we met one and the 64-pagers were the best we could find.

Right from the loud, brash and attractive covers to the closing catalogue of titles we hadn't yet read and the order form which agonizingly but appealingly had an American address, the 64-pagers promised and delivered something that could be matched only by the Sunday matinee in the Castle Cinema.

The fact that the comics originated – like the films – on the other side of the Atlantic – an ocean most of us had never seen, let alone ventured out on – made them even more exotic. They arrived in parcels from aunts and uncles and cousins. They returned in suitcases from England. They occasionally appeared at jumble sales in the local halls. They were that rarest of things in a small village – an outside influence. Word of the latest arrival was greeted with all the excitement of a new baby. Actually – if I'm honest – as far as we were concerned the 64-pager was much more interesting than any newly born brother or sister. And once the word was out, the offers came flooding in. Doors would be knocked, propositions would be made for the "lend" of the new arrival, the bidding war got underway. It was a competitive market and sometimes the currency varied. I once got the use of a penknife for a week in return for two 64-pagers. On the Saturday morning the comics were brought back and the penknife, which had lain hidden in the shed, to be taken out and looked at when my parents weren't around, was given back in a ceremony that had all the pomp and intensity of an international treaty.

I don't know how many sixty-four-pagers I got through but Kanter produced 167 of these gems, finishing with *Faust* in 1962, just about the time when I was becoming aware of their existence. That was the great thing about them: they might wear and tear but they were sturdier, in every way, than the weekly offerings that we picked up religiously from Mary Nolan's shop.

They had that intangible something that we imagined had to do with the size, the shape and the exotic covers. But what it had to do with really was the fact that these were classic stories made simple but never made trite. The quality of the illustrations varied and no doubt some of the authors might have revolved in their graves if they'd seen what had become of their precious work. But for me, a snotty-nosed ten-year-old, the world had stopped revolving for 64 pages. Huck Finn, Robinson Crusoe; Jekyll and Hyde; Robin Hood; Charles Dickens and Jack London were all available to me. Never mind that I didn't know fact from fiction; character from author; good drawing from bad. These were stories, adventures, tragedies and triumphs and when the sixty-four-pager had been read and re-read, there was that catalogue at the end with its promise of other adventures still to come.

Apple-Picking

When my father retired from his job on the railway, he tackled the garden with renewed energy. Spring and summer it was alive with digging and sowing and weeding and tending. Vegetables sprang up and thrived. He even ventured into growing – or "experimenting with" to use his own words – vegetables that until then he had treated as suspicious exotica.

The one thing he didn't have in the garden was an apple tree which is somewhat surprising because the house in which he and my mother first lived after their marriage had several apple trees. Add to that the fact that my father loved apples and apple tarts and it's even more surprising.

One late summer afternoon in the mid-seventies he arrived home all excited. He had met the wife of a farmer and she had told him he could come and take apples from their orchard. And so he did, returning with two shopping bags – one each of cookers and eaters. The smile on my father's face showed his delight with the yield, it shadowed the look that must have crossed Adam's face when he first encountered the magic fruit tree in that other garden.

And so the tradition was born. Twice a year, in late summer and late autumn, my father would take two shopping bags and drive to the farm; spend an afternoon collecting the apples and come back with his bag of cookers and his bag of eaters. Nothing tasted better, he said. No shop-bought apple could compare.

What I didn't discover until my father was well into his eighties was that he had been given permission, all those years before, to collect the windfalls in the orchard. He had never picked an apple from a tree. I was shocked and I was annoyed. We had words about it. How, I asked, could he allow someone to tell him he could only have the windfalls? The orchard was enormous. There must have been fifty trees there and many of the apples would rot on the sagging, overburdened branches. "That's not the point," he said. "Those people are decent enough to let me in, to let me collect what I want to collect. They don't stand over me and I don't take what's theirs."

We left it at that but the conversation came back to me recently, years after my father's death. It came back during a conversation about land and ownership and history. The anger welled up in me again, though I could almost hear my father's ghost at my shoulder, chiding me, telling me to leave well enough alone.

What my father saw was generosity – his being allowed to collect apples from someone else's orchard – and, of course, there was a generosity involved. But what I see is a man in his eighties trudging through the damp grasses of autumn afternoons in search of windfalls to fill his shopping bag.

What my father saw was the opportunity to harvest something that would otherwise have rotted on the ground, the chance to forage for food. He was an inland beachcomber, making something of nothing. But I see a man with his eyes downcast, bending beneath the heavily laden branches of full, ripe fruit, in search of the least bruised, least battered offerings of the wind.

And every time I think of him – and more and more these days I think of him – Robert Graves's sad and wonderful lines come into my head, those lines about the young bird-catcher who swept off his hat as the Squire's daughter rode by.

Harry Tully

"He's what's classed as a knight of the road," my father says.

We're driving through Hallahoise, on our way home from Athy. My father at the end of a day's work on the railway, myself at the end of a day's schooling. We've just passed Harry Tully, walking hunched in the opposite direction. Over his shoulder he carries a sack bag. His hat is brown and his threadbare coat catches the light of the evening sun.

Sometimes, in winter, my father picks up Harry on the road and takes him to Athy. He travels with us to the railway station and then walks the mile and a half to the County Home where he'll spend the darkest, coldest days of the year. On those mornings I sit in the back of the Morris Minor, waiting to hear him speak but he never says a word. He climbs in and out of the car in silence. His clothes smell of earth and hay and dampness.

"He can't help that," my father says. "He sleeps in fields a lot of the time or in haysheds and barns, so there's not much he can do about it. He's a harmless man. If everyone was as peaceable, the world would be a better place."

In summertime we often don't see Harry for weeks on end. He spends the warm months wandering the roads of Carlow, Kildare and west Wicklow, sleeping in places he hasn't slept in for a year. Sometimes, during the long summer holidays, he reappears, genuflecting arthritically and blessing himself as he passes the church in Castledermot, muttering at us brats as we call him names.

And then, as happens every year, the trees go on fire and drop their ashy leaves, and the last of the honeysuckle withers in the ditches, and a crust of frost appears on the morning windscreen, and my father curses and swings the starting handle to bring the car engine to life.

On one such wintry morning, there's Harry Tully at the bottom of Mullaghcreelan Hill, leaning against the parapet of the hump-backed bridge. My father stops the car and I peer through the back window as the old man comes shuffling like a hedgehog along the road.

He slumps heavily into the front seat, resting a moment before lifting his feet in after him and pulling the door closed. For a while his breath is cold in the warm car and then there's just the sound of his lungs sucking and battling against the season and the day. By the time we reach Grangenolvin, two miles down the road, Harry is asleep. I smell the smell again but I say nothing and then I catch my father's glance in the mirror as he checks the sleeping knight.

That morning we don't stop at the railway station. Instead, we drive to the County Home. My father leaves the old knight and myself in the car and goes inside the infirmary door. I'm terrified that Harry will wake but he doesn't. A minute later my father returns, followed by a nurse with a wheelchair. Together they help the old man out of the car and into the chair. He seems hardly to notice that he's been moved.

"I don't like the look of him," my father whispers to the nurse and then, realising I've overheard, he smiles and says: "But maybe he'll weather the storm."

I wait until we're beyond the gates of the County Home yard before asking the question.

"Is he going to die?"

My father doesn't answer for a couple of moments and when he does, his tone is calm and measured: "He might...he might."

But Harry doesn't die. My father rings the hospital the next day and the next.

"He's on the mend," he tells me. We're driving up Mullaghcreelan Hill, the last low beams of winter sunlight spearing the ditches. "He's a hardy old soul."

The following spring Harry Tully is on the road again and he raises his hand as we pass. My father waves back.

"Tough as nails," my father says and then he laughs. And I laugh, too.

Jude the Obscure

I loved being an altar boy. I loved the smell of incense and I particularly loved the high days of Christmas and Easter, the processions in May and at Corpus Christi; the October devotions when the church was all but empty and that wet and windy race between the dead priests' yawning graves to ring the outside bell on stormy nights. I loved the marriages and the funerals, the christenings and the churchings. There was a drama about these events; a euphoria and a sadness that were equal in the eye of the young boy I was back then.

And then there were the missions when we got to hear of the mysterious and exciting doings and misdoings of the adult world, particularly when the missioners spoke about the seventh and the tenth commandments – it was like being allowed into the Castle Cinema to see an over-18 film – and for free!

And always in this world of surplice and soutane – of incense and thurible; of ringing bells and statutes covered in purple cloths for Lent and daffodils exploding from their vases at Easter midnight mass – there was one steadfast figure who remained though Parish Priests and curates came and went – *the woman in black.*

It was she who came, early each morning, to unlock the sacristy and unbolt the main door and the doors to the women's and men's side aisles. It was she who was there last thing at night to slide the heavy bolts in place and turn the keys. And during Mass, she knelt in a pew halfway down the church, her black coat covering a black dress; her black stockings resting in deep black shoes; a black hat or mantilla covering her head.

We altar boys took her for granted – though there was something about her, an air of sadness, that we didn't understand and had no eagerness to intrude upon. None of us knew why she dressed as she did and none of us could be bothered to ask. All I knew was that her name was Mrs Dooley and that she lived somewhere up on Crop Hill, in the countryside above the village and our busy lives.

When you're eight or nine or even eleven or twelve, certain adults are there at the periphery of your life. You take them for granted, you have an occasional curiosity about them but, generally, they're of no great significance.

In 1974 I returned to Castledermot, as a young teacher in the local Technical School. My subjects were English and History and I set about writing a short social account of the locality. One of my sources of information was a glass case at the back of the church, at the end of the main aisle. Inside it, people had, over the decades, pinned memoriam cards of their loved ones. On October evenings, in the half-light of the empty church, I trawled through the cards – each one telling a life story. The occasional soldier from the Great War – written out of our history; deaths from the War of Independence; a frenzy of departures during the Great Flu of 1918 and 1919; children killed in accidents; the half-familiar faces of the parents and grandparents of my schoolmates and then, at the bottom of the case, I found a card with a photograph of a handsome young man called Dooley who had died at sea when the merchant ship on which he was serving was torpedoed during the Second World War. The address on the card was Crop Hill, Castledermot and I knew, intuitively, that he was the husband of *The Woman in Black*.

But only lately did I discover the woman's Christian name. Jude. She had – as was the habit of the time – dressed in black on learning of her husband's death at sea in 1942, but the mourning had continued for the rest of her days, decades spent in grief for the lost, lamented love of her life.

And we altar boys, seeing her as an old woman in the nineteen sixties, when in fact she was probably in her late forties or early fifties, had – with the callow innocence of childhood – missed one of the great lessons of our days, manifested in this woman whose life, even after her husband's death, had been linked inextricably with his. This woman who travelled several miles each morning to open the church doors and travelled the same miles each evening when the dark doors banged shut and spent her nights in the cottage she and her husband had shared for far too short a time. This Jude the Obscure who was there on the periphery of our lives, living in the shadows of time and loss; this woman who never gave up on the life she had dreamed, even after that dream had been extinguished.

The Last Irish Wolf

When I walk out my front door the first thing I see on the horizon is Mount Leinster, dominating the skyline, topped by the RTE mast. But even without the added height of the mast, the mountain is a substantial and impressive sight, soaring above the countryside of south County Carlow.

The mountain is many things to many people but to me it's for ever the home of the last Irish wolf and whenever I think of that animal I think of the sad and inevitable trail of destruction that followed the Irish wolf through the last two hundred years of its existence.

As far back as 1584, when the then Lord Deputy of Ireland began plotting the downfall of these wild and beautiful creatures, their days were numbered. He invited a man called Robert Legge to devise a plan to persuade people to help in the destruction of wolves. Over the following twenty-five years further legislation was introduced and the wolf became an unwanted animal in the Irish landscape.

By 1614 the price on a wolf's head was £3, making its extinction a financially rewarding business. For the native Irish, the wolf had long been a prey but there had never been an attempt to wipe out the population – it was more a case of live and let live. But for the English in Ireland, the wolf was a threat and a nuisance – particularly in the wake of the Cromwellian wars and, with the arrival of professional wolf hunters from England and the introduction of a ban on the export of wolfhounds from the country, the killing of wolves became a serious and lucrative business.

By 1652 the bounty on wolves had risen to £6 for a female and £5 for a male and ten shillings for a cub. Thousands of pounds were paid out in rewards for the destruction of the wolves. By the end of the seventeenth

149

century wolves appear to have been extinct in Ulster and were under severe pressure elsewhere. The last record of a wolf kill was on the side of Mount Leinster in 1786, when an animal was hunted and destroyed for killing sheep. That wolf was the last of its kind and it must have felt an extraordinary and terrifying sense of isolation as its pack grew smaller and smaller and, finally, disappeared.

Wolves are social animals. They live and hunt in groups. The Irish name for the wolf is Mac Tire – son of the countryside. For this last son or daughter of the Irish countryside there was nowhere left to run. Big as the mountain was, it wasn't big enough to provide a place of concealment from the humans who had decided there wasn't sufficient room for it and them in south County Carlow.

For that last of its kind in Ireland, the landscape was nothing more than a place in which to try to hide; a place to chase down a meal; a place to survive for as long as survival was possible. Surviving is not living. Gone were the comfort and support of the pack; gone was the possibility of breeding; gone was the companionship of other wolves. And gone was the tradition of thirty-four thousand years – the tradition of the Morrigan taking on the form of a wolf as she struggled with Cú Chulainn; the tradition – akin to that of Romulus and Remus – that Cormac MacAirt was raised by wolves; the tale of the priest who encountered a talking wolf – a human under a spell as it happened – and was persuaded to give the man's wife, also trapped in wolf form, the last rites before she died.

Wolves don't have human sentiment but, like all animals, they have a keen sense of survival and a keen sense of danger and an intense sense of terror when their lives are threatened. And they also have an understanding of isolation and loneliness. That last wolf, harried and hunted across the flanks of Mount Leinster, must have had some sense that its life was, at the very least, in great and immediate danger.

What it didn't know was that it was the last of its race in Ireland. That is something we know and something that crosses my mind every time I drive or walk the roads and paths that criss-cross that great mountain. And, when animals call in the night, I can't help but think of that last wolf calling – for companionship; for consolation; for survival; for assistance. A call that came too late.

Learning to Dance

There's something about the taste of toothpaste and the smell of floor polish that remind me of boarding school. The floor polish is obvious. Each autumn, as we walked through the front door of St Clement's College in Limerick, the smell that met us was of freshly waxed and polished floors. The tiles gleamed in the September afternoons and whatever light was in the sky caught the sparkle and danced it back at us.

And then there's the taste of the toothpaste, the sharp, minty taste that transports me to the dormitory and the sounds of laughter and the silence that fell the moment the doors swung open and the priest on duty began his nightly rounds.

Once I'd settled in, I loved boarding school. I enjoyed the comradeship; enjoyed the plays, the debating and the fraternity of the boys who were my fellow students. In theory, we were all potential priests and the school was intended to take us in that direction, but what we got was a full and rounded and liberal education. Perhaps that was because I arrived in the wake of Vatican II when doors were opening and new ideas were part of our daily lives.

Not that my first three months at St Clement's were always a joy. I was desperately lonely and the fact that my brother had been there before me didn't make life any easier. He was well remembered, for his academic prowess and for his stage presence. He had been the Pirate King in *The Pirates of Penzance* in his final year.

I remember driving the hours from Kildare to Limerick in the Morris Minor to see and hear him on stage. He looked ten feet tall in his pirate outfit, a huge feathered hat on his head, a sword in his hand. I was as proud as punch of him and I think that was the night I began to believe that nothing bad would ever happen to me as long as he was around.

When I first arrived at St Clement's, I wondered how he had survived and whether I ever could. Our French teacher told us daily that *the first seven years are the worst, gentlemen*, and insisted on reminding me that my brother's shadow fell heavily on my shoulders.

By the time I'd reached fifth year, I walked with my own shadow behind me – walked and ran and played football and basketball but, like my sixteen class comrades, I had never learned to dance. And then, unexpectedly, a new light shone into our sheltered lives. To our amazement – this being an all-boys, all-boarders, Redemptorist Juniorate with less than a hundred pupils and just one female teacher – our Reverend headmaster informed us that we would be having dancing lessons from Miss Sylvia Leigh-Doyle and we were to behave ourselves like the gentlemen he was endeavouring to make of us! Our expectations were of a starchy, prim and proper lady in tweeds who would bark if we were out of step. Instead, a young, slim, athletic woman appeared in the common room. We were in awe of her. Collectively, unanimously and instantly, the seventeen of us fell in love. And in that magic number – seventeen – lay the path to the fulfilment of our dreams. Seventeen boys learning to waltz, each with a male partner from the class, left an odd-man-out every week and that odd-man-out got to dance with Sylvia Leigh-Doyle.

My turn came and my turn went, my heart hammering in my chest; my eyes glued to the floor, trying to keep control of my two left feet. We twirled, she and I, to Engelbert Humperdinck's *The Last Waltz*. For this was another great thing about Sylvia Leigh-Doyle: she didn't bring in Strauss records for our dancing lessons, she brought in music we knew and loved. And among the bundle of singles and albums she deposited beside the radiogram was *Parsley, Sage, Rosemary and Thyme*. Sometimes, when our dancing came to an early halt, she's let us listen to her records in the common room. I was engrossed by several of the tracks on the Simon and Garfunkel album but particularly by "For Emily Whenever I May Find Her."

On our last day before the Easter holidays I was listening to the album, gently replacing the stylus for the fifth time at the start of track 4 on side 2 when a voice at my shoulder said, "You seem to like that song."

"I like the whole album," I stammered.

"Well why don't you take it home with you for the Easter holidays?"

"Are you serious?"

"Absolutely. Take it with you."

Despite her best efforts, I didn't learn to dance but I learned to revere the songs of Paul Simon and I got to borrow Sylvia Leigh-Doyle's album for ten days and went on being in love with its owner for the rest of that year.

We Were Boys Then

It may be the way the leaves are beginning to rust on the trees or it may be the psychedelic rainbows of dahlias in the early September gardens. Perhaps it's the way the evening light has begun to withdraw, like a shy student, but, to be honest, I think it's a whiff of floor polish that I caught somewhere, that distinct, institutional smell, that whispered *school* in my ear.

This time last year we had a reunion in the old school – St Clement's College in Limerick. It was a warm, sociable occasion – the class of 1970 – all miraculously still alive and kicking.

And before the reunion Mass, before the meal and the recollections, the tall tales and the white lies, we walked through the old school building, still standing but superseded now by a new and shining school to the rear. The blueprint of memory was the same – the empty classrooms with their echoes of rote – *mensa, mensa, mensam* and *alpha, beta, gamma, delta, epsilon, zeta, eta, theta, iota, kappa, lambda, moo, noo, ksi, omicron, pi, ro, sigma, tau, upsilon, phi, kee, psi, omega*; the dormitories with the lost music of late-night Radio Luxembourg on smuggled earphones beneath the sheets; the refectory – still redolent with the scent of warm custard on hard tack; the common room alive with the murmur of newspapers and the latest singles from Savin's record shop on O'Connell Street; the boot room vibrant with ghost boys ducking from ricocheting footballs; the study hall where we learned, among other arts, the skill of disguising a comic book as an atlas.

Indeed, the architecture of the building was much the same as it had been when we stepped, uncertainly, through the front door and into the hallway on that September afternoon in 1965, but the smell was different – there was no scent of floor polish, nothing of the fragrance that greeted us each term on our return, not an iota of the perfume that followed us down those corridors when, finally, we left in the wake of our Leaving Cert in the June of 1970.

While we walked, each of us seemed lost in our personal reminiscences, recalling those green but determined aspirations; the hopes we nurtured; the ambitions we treasured. I was catching the resonance of the vibrant, half-baked arguments we'd had about God and life and politics and the world and what needed changing and how we were the ones who could make those changes. For some of us, the mission fields of Africa and South America were the target; for others, the aim was to be civil servants or teachers; for some, the lure was to return to the farms and fields and hay-sheds that had never lost their fascination.

Finally, we closed the door behind us and stepped into the garden that is changed now, the garden that housed the handball alleys and the tarmac soccer pitch and the basketball gym and the forever unfinished swimming pool. And I thought of all the young men and women stepping through the doors of schools and colleges and places of learning and of the sights, the sounds and the smells that will greet them. And I remembered the twenty young men who had come together in Limerick so long ago, travelling from all corners of Ireland and from America, melding into a family for the five years we shared and carrying with us a kind of brotherhood that has outlasted time. And I wrote these lines:

We were boys then,

filled with the expectation of the age,

fired by the vastness of the desert,

by the voice in the burning bush,

156

by the cross on the peak of the crooked hill.

But now we are these other people,

not the ghosts our fathers were,

not old before our years.

We are something else,

men trapped between a time that was

and a future without certainty.

What do we wish for ourselves?

Long life and happiness,

the peace to be at ease with what we've done or not undone,

some morsel from the plate of youth,

the will to stay forever open to the possibilities of life and love,

of the time we call tomorrow.

And tonight?

Perhaps, tonight we wish, beyond all else,

for the gift of memory,

the strength to face the wilderness

and not allow our fearlessness become our fear.

A way to be the boys we were back then.

Mick Carolan

This afternoon the players from two teams will take the field in Croke Park, men in search of the greatest prize Gaelic football has to offer – an All-Ireland medal.

By tea time – barring a draw – the players from one side will have the precious metal in their hands, they'll have walked back across the hallowed turf, as the autumn evening falls, feeling thirty feet tall; they'll have been part of the mayhem that is the winners' dressing room; some of them will have sat quietly, savouring the hour; others will be overflowing with energy, whooping it up like there's no tomorrow. Backs will be slapped, hands shaken, tears will fall, laughter will echo along the corridors and out onto the deserted field and the empty stands.

And, for others, the dream will, at best, have been postponed.

For me, All-Ireland final mornings bring thoughts of those monumental footballers who never won that ultimate prize and each of us will have our own list of men whose ability and skill we admired, even in defeat. My list includes the great Dermot Earley of Roscommon; Mickey Kearns of Sligo; Kevin O'Brien of Wicklow; Willie Quinlan of Carlow; Glen Ryan and Anthony Rainbow of Kildare – men whose playing days were days of wonder, whose ability wove spells, who truly were the magicians in my life.

I still live in hope of seeing Johnny Doyle and Dermot Earley Junior lift the Sam Maguire for Kildare but of the men who deserved to but never did, there's one man who stands above all others in my mind.

He was a colossus – a half-back on the Kildare teams between 1957 and 1975; a winner of Railway Cup medals with Leinster; an All Star in 1966; a man who played and lost in four Leinster Finals and two national league finals. He was the epitome of a brilliant, committed, talented and sublime footballer, he never won a provincial or an All-Ireland medal, yet he was a man who never stopped believing.

My particular memories of him come from opposite ends of his career.

The first is of a summer Sunday, in the early sixties. Kildare were playing in a championship match in Athy and the ground was crammed with supporters. The huxters were flaunting the *hats, colours and ribbons* – crepe paper hats that ran in the rain; the *Luckie Luckies* – Lucan ice-creams – were on sale outside the gate. Inside, we were urged to get *the last of the choc ices* before the ball had even been thrown in, and the same cry was still going up as the final whistle approached.

There were no fences or security gates back then, children sat on their fathers' shoulders or squatted on the side-line, as close as could be to the action. And that's where I found myself, cross-legged, close to the half-way line, my flag – a rip of old sheet stuck with drawing pins to a piece of stick – in my hand. At that level, every kick was heard and every tackle was felt and every shoulder made the ground shudder. And, above all others, one player dominated the sky and the ground that afternoon; one man rose to field every high ball and to launch attack after attack from the half-back line. That man was Mick Carolan. To me he was everything I wanted to be. Tall, handsome, athletic, fearless, talented. He was Kildare.

When the heavy, laced football thudded out of play beside me and he came to take a sideline kick, I was as close to him as I'd ever been, so close that I must have been in his line of fire but, instead of asking me to move, he reached down and ruffled my hair before steadying himself and putting the ball over the bar. Had the hand of God reached from the clouds and anointed me, I wouldn't have felt any more deeply or wonderfully blessed.

I had been anointed by the touch of greatness.

Years later, in 1998, when Kildare reached the All-Ireland final, I wrote about that incident and a couple of days later I got a phone call, asking if I could meet Mick Carolan. Can a bird fly? Can an elephant remember? Of course I could meet him and I did. And he brought me a gift – the jersey he'd worn in the 1958 league final – he might as well have given me the Shroud of Turin.

So when the teams launch themselves onto the pitch in Croke Park this afternoon, I'll be sparing a thought for the gifted players who have never won the Sam Maguire – Earley, Quinlan, Kearns, O'Brien and – above all others – the great Mick Carolan.

The Crest of a White Wave

From a long time ago and a great distance away, names and faces find their way back through the emptying stadiums of memory.

Ask me about the spring or the early summer of 1998 and I'll tell you I remember very little. I moved house, planted a new garden, built dry stone walls and travelled to see Kildare play Dublin in the Leinster Senior Football quarter-final. Travelled as I had done for forty years, as Kildare supporters always do, with faith but without certainty; with insecurity but not entirely devoid of hope, that strange coagulation of the footballing blood that is part of our DNA.

The previous year had been a case of almost but not quite. A thirteen-man Kildare, managed by Mick O'Dwyer, had beaten Laois and taken Meath to two replays before going down, so none of us knew what the new season might hold.

On the first Sunday in June 1998, we drew with Dublin. It looked as though we might never get across the starting line, let alone the finishing line. Forty-two years without a Leinster title stretched behind us like an empty road on a winter evening. Two weeks later we were back in Croke Park and nosed home by a point in a game that was tense to the bitter end.

Four weeks would pass before we faced Laois on the same pitch – these were the days when there were no back doors. You went through the front door of victory or you stayed away. This time we strolled home – 2.13 to eight point winners. And suddenly it was the first Sunday in August and there were the lilywhites running out onto Croke Park to face Meath in a Leinster final.

My memories of that afternoon are that we seemed to have it won but

Meath – as ever – refused to lie down and suddenly the dream was enveloped in the shadows of a nightmare. Trevor Giles, Tommy Dowd and Jody Devine took their points and it looked as though the forty-two-year wait would stretch to at least another year. And then it happened – Brian Murphy took a pass from Martin Lynch in the dying minutes and drove it past the Meath defence and into the Hill 16 goal. When the final whistle sounded, we had won by five points and the stands drained like a ruptured milk tanker and a wash of white flooded across the pitch and Glen Ryan sang "The Curragh of Kildare" and there among the crowd of faces was Dermot Earley Senior, who had managed Kildare before Mick O' Dwyer's second coming, and we shook hands and I thanked him for the work he'd put in and the wave of white rolled back and forth across the pitch and the sun was dipping before we hit the Naas Road, still euphoric, still not quite believing.

Four weeks later we were back in Croke Park, beating Kerry by a point, reaching an All-Ireland final which now filled our every waking and sleeping moment.

The last Sunday in September dawned grey and overcast. I was on crutches. The night before, my son, Ewan, and myself had played our own version of the Kildare Galway match on the lawn – a season-long tradition – and I had torn ligaments in fielding a high ball. I should have read the omens but we were going into the game having beaten the 1995, '96 and '97 champions *en route* so even I, the eternal pessimist, had hope.

The match itself is something I still shudder to remember. There was the injury that Glen Ryan carried onto the field; there was the wonderful but ultimately false dawn of the first half; there was Dermot Earley's goal which gave us a three-point half-time lead; there was Padraic Joyce's goal that put the Tribesmen back in control and, from there to the end, try as the

Kildare might, we couldn't catch them. The final whistle saw Galway clear by four and suddenly the seats around us were empty as their supporters streamed down the aisles and onto the pitch.

Ewan sat hunched beside me, unable to speak, his body convulsing in spasms of tears and desolation. I was no better. I had dared to believe, as the summer grew into autumn, that the unimaginable might happen, that the seventy-year wait for an All-Ireland might end.

And then I saw an elderly Galway man, who had been making his way down the steps towards the pitch, stop and watch us for a moment before slowly climbing back up and edging along the row of seats until he stood behind us. Gently he placed a big, work-hardened hand on each of our shoulders, leaned over and said, very quietly: "Always, always be proud of your county."

From a long time ago and a great distance away, names and faces and voices find their way back through the deserted stadiums of memory and his is one of the clearest and most treasured.

Robbing Orchards

For Keats, this may have been the season of mist and mellow fruitfulness but for us, growing up in Castledermot in the 1960s, it was the season for robbing orchards. Never mind that there were apple trees and apples galore at the bottom of our parents' gardens – the stolen apple was always the sweetest.

And so it was that four of us set out one Sunday afternoon to rob a certain orchard that held its own challenge – *the greater the danger, the greater the achievement* was our motto, even if we couldn't as eleven-year-olds quite articulate it. The particular challenge of this orchard, situated to the side of a substantial farmhouse about two miles out from the village, was that the owners had built their latrine right in the middle of the orchard, so robbing the apples involved the possibility of being caught by someone who saw us from the house or by someone already ensconced in the WC.

This latrine was about the size of a confession box and had a solid wooden door with a small glass window above it, to let in some light but too high up for us to know whether the facility was occupied or not. It also had a corrugated iron roof, and on past orchard-robbing forays we had scouted the area by tossing rocks onto this roof and waiting to hear a response or none from within. Once, the landing of the rocks had been followed by a loud female scream and we had scarpered.

But, on that autumn Sunday afternoon in 1964, after the rocks had clattered on the corrugated roof there was only silence. The coast was clear. We headed for the sweetest apples and I was delegated to climb into the branches and throw down the fattest and juiciest fruits to my companions waiting below, small jute sacks in their hands.

I had thrown no more than half-a-dozen apples to my accomplices when one of them noticed the door of the latrine opening slowly and quietly. "Run!" he shouted and run they did, clearing the ditch like thoroughbreds and leaving me high and dry, stranded on the tallest branch.

The farmer, to whom the orchard belonged, ambled calmly across the grass.

"I can see you up there," he said.

I was silent.

"Jesse James," he said. "But it looks like the rest of the James Boys have scattered and left you to the sheriff."

Still not a word from me.

"I recognise you," he said. "You're the young Mac Kenna fellow. Your mother is the teacher."

The game was very definitely up.

I climbed gingerly down, trying not to disturb the apples as I descended. And then I was standing in his shadow. He looked ten feet tall, a solid man in his Sunday suit.

"Now," he said quietly, "you have two choices. I can drive you home and tell your mother and father what you were up to and you can take the consequences. Or..." and he paused for emphasis..." or I can give you a good solid kick in the arse and you can go about your business. The choice is yours."

I didn't have to think about it for very long. My mother would not be pleased and the fact that this sturdy farmer was also a member of the Church of Ireland would bring double shame on the family. I could hear her already: "Haven't I warned you often enough not to be hanging around with that lot. And of all the orchards to steal from ... what must they think of us!" And that would just be for starters.

There really was no choice.

In the distance I spotted my three co-conspirators walking slowly across the headland of a field, ready to climb a gate and make their way back home, free and doubtless already planning which orchard to rob next.

"Well?" the farmer asked.

"I'll take the kick in the arse," I said resignedly.

"Fair enough. A wise choice, I'd say. And I just want to add that this will give me great pleasure and cause you a fair deal of pain."

And he was right. It was a solid kick from a solid man and it sent me a good three or four feet on my way. After that I just ran but, painful and all as the experience was, I knew – just as he did – that I'd made the right decision.

The Little Green Man

In the corner of the garden that was childhood's garden, I made a graveyard. I can't deny it – I had a mania for death in my childhood. I think that was the main attraction in being an altar boy: the opportunity to attend funerals. And as for wakes, I was first into the car whenever there was talk of one. I think I missed my calling – undertaking would have suited me down to the ground, and six-feet under it.

Anything that died was buried in that garden graveyard – pinkeens, butterflies, wasps, rabbits and the Little Green Man. In summertime the funerals were mainly for pinkeens. We'd catch them in the brook and they'd survive for a couple of days in jam-jars on the windowsill outside the back door. One survived for three weeks and a day. That was a record. The cruelty of children is often unknown to them.

That particular pinkeen was what we called a Black Doctor, because of its black underbelly. There were Red Doctors, too – prized little fish, seldom caught and all the more highly valued for that. Joe Whelan, from next door, was the undertaker when we buried the three-week-and-a-day pinkeen. I was the priest – that was the routine we'd worked out. I think Joe was always wary of things ecclesiastical. On that summer afternoon, he solemnly carried the Calvita box, which held the limp little fish, while I placed an old scarf of my mother's around my neck – this was to be my stole. I had served at enough funerals to know the drill.

At the graveside, a ten-inch hole we'd dug on the narrow patch of untilled ground near the bottom hedge, I sprinkled water from a jam-jar on the box and intoned some ill-formed Latin words: *Pater noster, ave Maria, benedictus, sanctus, nostris, panis angelicus, tantum ergo. Amen.* And then

I delivered the sermon, doing my best to replicate the kind of thing I'd heard in the church. *This man was a great man. He lived a good life. He leaves behind a wife and twenty children who have no money and no food. We pray for them for ever and ever. Amen.*

"It's only a bloody pinkeen," Joe said. "Get on with it." It was late morning and he was hungry I think. Anyway, I ignored him.

We stretched two pieces of twine beneath the Calvita box and lowered it into the hole. Joe shovelled in the clay – using a dessert spoon we'd borrowed from our kitchen. That done, we made a cross from two sticks and the now redundant twine, a cross just like all the other crosses that littered that patch of the garden.

Sometimes, when pinkeens were scarce and wasps were out of season, I'd bury the Little Green Man. He was a plastic figure with a steering wheel in his hands, survivor of some long-lost red toy racing car that had gone to its own reward in the great scrapyard in the sky. I'd bury him often but I always marked the burial spot well so I could dig him up and reuse him. He was the Lazarus of my undertaking obsession!

When we moved house in 1958 – all the way across the football field from one Abbeylands to another – the Green Man travelled with me. I buried him in the new garden, beneath the sitting-room window. It was on the October day when Pope Pius XII was being buried in Rome. My mother was listening to the funeral on the radio in the sitting-room and I could hear the commentary through the open window. For once, there was someone else to supply the words and the Vatican choir sang the Latin hymns, the voices rising in the still air of the autumn afternoon.

What I hadn't bargained for was what happened a week or two later. My father decided he was going to lay a concrete path across the front of the house, a path that ran past the hall door and beneath the sitting room window. The path was put in one Saturday while I was away playing football and, by the time I got back home, the Little Green Man had disappeared beneath a foot of concrete, never to be resurrected. Even Lazarus, I realised, had had his day!

John MacKenna

The Nature of Friendship

I turned on the radio one evening recently to hear Joni Mitchell singing about the last time she saw Richard, in Detroit in '68. And it reminded me of the first time I saw Richard. It was in Limerick in September '66. I was halfway down the main stairs in St Clement's College and he was coming through the front doorway with his parents. He was a new arrival and I was a second-year-man-of-the-world. And that was the beginning of a friendship that still follows its own heartbeat more than fifty years later.

In the decades that followed, we travelled through secondary school and college together; on days when we might have been more, or less, productively employed at study, we played world-cup matches on the back pitch at Belfield; we discussed the possibility of living a hippy life on one of the Blasket Islands but never did; we shared work and lodgings in London in the burning summers of 1975 and 1976; we haunted the Royal Court Theatre, just across the road from our place of employment; we read the same books and spent long nights discussing the meanings of poems and the directions of our lives. Our friendship grew and deepened and our shared love of literature and theatre kept it singing.

And if you asked me now, more than fifty years into that friendship, what it is I best remember of the years gone by, I'd go back to a winter night at the end of January 1972. Paul Simon had just released his album *Paul Simon* and Richard and myself had spent the evening in the sitting-room of my parents' house in Castledermot, listening and relistening to the tracks –from "Mother and Child Reunion" through "Everything Put Together Falls Apart" to the closing notes of "Congratulations." No line went without analysis and no song was heard simply for its melody. The

170

love of words that had drawn us together was at the heart of the things we talked about as the LP spun on the turntable.

Eventually, late in the evening, my parents let it be known that they might just like to watch some programme or other on TV and Richard and I pulled on our jackets and headed out into the night. Castledermot in 1972 did not possess a coffee-shop – it didn't even lay claim to a chip shop – so we set off walking and did the circle that took us out the pitch-dark Barrack Road, past the towering shadow of Prumplestown Mill and back in the Carlow Road – a walk of four or five miles. It was late – well after midnight – when we ambled down Barn Hill, past the frozen greens of the pitch and putt club. And that was when we had the idea. We would attempt to walk from one end of the village, from Farrelly's bicycle shop, to Behan's garage at the other end but without stepping off the white lines – broken and unbroken – that ran along the middle of what was then the main Dublin to Waterford road. If a car or lorry disturbed us then the adventure would be deemed a failure, if we made it, it would be a night to remember.

And so we walked, crossing the Lerr Bridge, past the ruined abbey and the closed doors of the Castle Cinema; beneath the shadow of Joan of Arc's statue in Aylmer's garden; by the national schools, with the immense shadow of the round tower behind them; across the Square and on and on, passing Hennessy's garage and the moonlit remnants of the plague hospital until, finally, the white line disappeared where the road passed Behan's garage and stretched away by the cottages at Skenagun and on, into the buttermilk distance of open countryside. We had done it – not a solitary car had disturbed our walk, not a lorry or van had interrupted our conversation. We had, in the space of half an hour, passed a thousand years of history and a lifetime of analysis; we had settled on an interpretation of "Mother and Child Reunion"; we had discussed the irony in "Congratulations" and we had agreed that "Peace Like a River" had something magical about it, something that reflected the wonder and delight of our little voyage along that narrow white line, in the middle of a deserted but moonlit road in a tiny Kildare village.

In the forty-five years since that night, our lives have broken in different directions. Sometimes a year passes between meetings but all I have to do is slip that Paul Simon album into the CD player, skip to track 7 and I'm back on the moon-drenched road, the night is still, the stars are frozen solid against the sky, the ghosts of centuries past have stepped away from the windows of empty buildings and Richard and myself are walking, lost in conversation, adrift in the moment, and I recognise, again and am reminded – if I need reminding – of the true and simple nature of our friendship.

Night Games

Sometimes things come together. Recently, I was driving on a cold, frosty night, stars shivering in the black sky, the moon long forgotten. And then REM's *Night Swimming* came on the radio and I was back in winter nights of childhood, nights when we were allowed stay out until seven or eight, nights when the darkness was our playground.

Inevitably the darkness and the novelty drew us to the football field, which sat then, as it still does, behind a stand of fir trees just across the road from where we lived. And there the night games would begin. There was something about playing football or hurling with just the light of one street lamp tattooing the grass with the odd shapes of branches, something about the gloom behind the goals that made the matches all the better. When the sliotar or the football disappeared into murk, the search began and might go on for ten minutes before the match could start again.

But for me the pleasure came from more than the darkness. It came from the tenuous connection I made between my scrapbook of photographs of soccer goalkeepers making impossible saves on frozen grounds around Europe. In these pictures I glimpsed something I had never seen – pitches lit by floodlights, huge, beautiful towering masses of steel topped with twenty or thirty burning lamps. And it wasn't that these floodlights made day of night – that wasn't the thrill. The thrill came from the fact that they opened the winter nights to life. The impossible was possible.

In our back yard there was a garage which my father had built in 1959, the year after we moved into the house. It had no door but it housed our Morris Minor and, later, the Austin A40 and it was the ideal goal for night games when there was no one else about. By bouncing a ball off the wall between the kitchen and bathroom windows, I could head it goal-wards. It needed a clean strike to carry it across the line and only clean strikes counted. Occasionally, when the ball hit the window instead of the wall, there'd be a rap on the glass and a *Careful* but, mostly, the European Cup matches went uninterrupted.

Yet the garage wasn't the real thing. The football field was the real thing and the football field in snow was even better. The snow magnified the weak light from the street lamp and suddenly the three or four of us who braved the elements were no longer playing three-goals-in, we were in full flight down the wing of some unpronounceable stadium in Russia and the crowd was out of their seats and the lights were burning above us and the snow beneath our hobnail boots was nothing because we could turn on a sixpence, jink like a coil and score from thirty yards, the sodden football rising above the flailing arms of the stranded keeper who had slipped and landed on his backside.

Never mind that the arguments would begin about the ball being wide – no nets to prove otherwise; or about someone being offside – a rule none of us understood but one we often invoked; or that the argument would then degenerate into name-calling because none of us had actually kept an eye on where the ball had gone.

And so it would go until one or other of us was called in. Sometimes, not often but sometimes, I was last to be called and those were the nights I loved best. Then I could weave and dive, turn and shoot and know that the goals I scored would count, know that the crowd was cheering for me, only me; know that when, finally, I collected the heavy leather ball and traipsed with frost-burnt fingers and soggy socks across the slushy pitch and over the wall at the edge of the field, I was bringing home the trophy and the glory and the pleasure of true happiness.

Recently, I passed the football pitch in Castledermot. It was a cold, crisp January night and the players were training under the startling beams of powerful floodlights. I stopped the car, got out, leaned on the wall and watched for a couple of minutes. And then I got back in and drove away. I didn't envy them the bright lights and the new clubhouse. Why would I? But, perhaps, for just a moment, I envied them their youth.

The Holyhead Train

The last week of August 1975, my friend Richie and myself are on the train to Holyhead. It's a Friday afternoon and we're planning to catch the night boat back to Ireland. The end of another summer spent working in the Royal Court Hotel in Sloane Square, London. A summer of reading Leonard Cohen's poetry and Salinger's *Raise High the Roof Beams, Carpenters*. A summer of saving money and living in a small, hot room that might have been our last when one of the other hotel workers tried to burn the place down one night. A summer of art galleries and waiting in Piccadilly Circus for love to find us under the blind eyes of Eros, and walking down Portobello Road for miles and seeing films that might never be released in Ireland. A summer of music dominated by 10CC's single *I'm not in Love* and Rod Stewart's *Atlantic Crossing* LP.

It's a month since the Miami Showband massacre and the five deaths on that night and it's two weeks since the deaths of five people in a bar on the Shankhill Road and just a couple of days after the bombing of Oxford Street in London which injures seven people. It's not a good time to be Irish in England and we haven't long settled into our train seats before a man and, later, a woman sit opposite. Like us, they're in their early twenties.

As the train pulls clear of London, the man engages us in conversation and, once he discovers we're Irish, the jokes begin. Not particularly funny and mildly irritating but we grin and bear them – I suppose we don't feel the need to defend ourselves. But the jokes are just the prelude to a more robust and vitriolic attack on most things Irish – from our dependence on England for work, to our unwillingness to become involved in the Second

World War to the indiscriminate bombing and killing of people on what our travelling companion describes as "the mainland."

"Why can't you people just get on with killing each other, if that's what you want to do?" he asks. Heads begin to turn. "I mean I don't mind you coming here to work but I want to be able to trust the people I work with, don't I? I mean I don't want to be looking at your luggage and wondering if it's going to explode and blow me to kingdom come, do I?"

We say nothing but silence is not the answer.

The man goes on, reminding us, again, that we've been collecting English wages, which is all well and fine if we don't then turn round and try to kill innocent people. That, he tells us, is the lowest of the low. Only venomous snakes stoop that low and he doesn't want them slithering and crawling out of the Irish Sea, dragging bags of Semtex behind them.

And that is when the young woman seated beside him puts down her book and turns to him and says with a polite but steely certainty: "I think you should shut up now." And, to my amazement, he does. Not another word until he departs at Crewe, with a five-letter farewell that is aimed, we agree, despite the anatomical implications, at all three of us.

And then we get talking. The young woman is from London but she's travelling to Llandudno to visit her grandmother. We swop stories about college, about music, about books, about jobs and about London. We list the films and exhibitions and plays we've seen that summer. Richie tells her how poor a play *Loot* is and how it was a waste of time and money even crossing Sloane Square to see it at the Royal Court Theatre. She tells us about the places we might have gone; the free concerts we should have seen; the music we could have heard at St Martin in the Fields. We laugh a lot and she tells us how much she'd like to visit Ireland and we tell her the "do's" and "don't's" of the country we call home.

Flint, Prestatyn, Rhyl, Colwyn Bay – the towns pass like poems. We buy coffee and cakes and talk about the important things in our green lives and then the train begins to slow again and the young woman smiles and says this is her station. I carry her bag the length of the carriage, the brakes scream like angle grinders and we clatter to a stop in Llandudno. She steps from the open door to the platform below and I step down and place her bag beside her. She rummages in it and produces a box of chocolates.

"For you," she says. "To prove we're not all full of hate."

"You don't have to prove anything," I say.

"Well just for you, then."

She smiles a very gentle smile, seems about to speak again, but hesitates.

A porter comes along the platform, slamming doors and whistling. I step back inside the carriage and he bangs the door between us. I open the window and lean out. The platform is almost deserted now, the shadows cutting shapes on the sun-soaked concrete.

"You could get off this train," the girl says quickly. "You could get off, here, now... with me."

I didn't get off the train. Instead, I watched the girl out of sight and she watched me.

Possibilities. Decisions. Consequences. Youth and uncertainty. All the "if's" and "might's" and "maybe's". But something of that moment has remained with me for thirty-six years; a moment – not in a yellow wood but on a sunny, railway station platform – where two choices diverged and the rest ... the rest is a large part of that space we call a life.

The Black Spider

I was in a clothes shop a few years ago – which is, in itself, a minor miracle – but more amazingly still there it was. A t-shirt with a photograph of Lev Yashin, the great Soviet goalkeeper – the Black Spider – on the top right-hand side of the chest. And beneath this picture of Yashin, palming the ball around the post, was a short biography. I had to produce my glasses to read the text but when I did, it raised a smile. Not only was the Black Spider – probably the best goalkeeper the world has ever seen – my hero but it transpired that we shared a birth date – 22 October. He'd been born a couple of decades ahead of me but the date was a bonus for the boy inside who had gone through hell and high water to incorporate the 'keepers name into his own.

It was the spring of 1965 and I was preparing to make my confirmation. The catechism was being studied; the questions that the Archbishop might throw at me in the church were being rehearsed with Brother Sinnott; the "do's" and "don't's" of the day were being gone through; we'd even been taken down to the Parish Church to acclimatise to the surroundings.

At home, at night, my mother drilled me again in the likely questions John Charles McQuaid might have for me. None of us lads in sixth class wanted to face the ignominy of not knowing the answer. There were whispered rumours that "someone" in the "not too distant past" had "failed the Archbishop's exam, on the day of his confirmation, in the church" and the self-same "someone" had had to slink out the side door and been "cast into eternal damnation – well he had to go home anyway in his new trousers and tell his mother he failed and he got a batin' from his father."

We were terrified and petrified by this news and we redoubled our efforts to learn the answers to every possible combination and complication that might be thrown our way.

I was well on target when the question of my confirmation name came up.

"What name are you taking?" my mother asked.

"Yashin," I said.

I'd already thought about this – there was no contest. It had to be Yashin. I had a scrapbook of photos of him; I'd cut out every account I could find in the newspapers of his great saves; every time I stepped onto the football pitch or the lawn or caught a high ball off the back wall of the house, I was Yashin.

"You can't take that name," my mother said. "You have to take a Saint's name!"

"Why?"

"Because you do. It's Confirmation, you can't just pick any name."

"I'm not. It's a real name. It's his name. He was baptised that name… well he was baptised Lev but Yashin is his family name."

I heard my father chuckle from behind his newspaper.

"He wasn't baptised," my mother said. "He's a communist. It's a communist name."

"So?"

"Get yourself out of that one," my father said quietly.

And my mother did – she passed the problem on to Brother Sinnott, who seemed not to have such a problem with Yashin, the name, or Yashin, the communist, as with the fact that he was a soccer goalkeeper. Brother Sinnott was from Wexford and hurling was his game. Soccer didn't appear on his sporting radar.

"Would you not take the name of a hurler – or even a footballer?" he asked.

"But, sir, Yashin is the best goalkeeper in the world, honestly, sir."

"Would he stop a sliotar?" Brother Sinnott asked.

We were standing in the empty classroom; the other boys were playing in the yard.

"Would he stop a pile driver from Nicky Rackard? Not a hope. Anyone can stop the big ball; it's the small ball that's the real man to make you hop."

"But he doesn't play hurling, sir."

"And do you know why not?" Brother Sinnott asked. "Because he wouldn't be up to it. He'd be put back in his box. He'd be seen for what he is. You want to think again about this name; you don't want to be taking the name of a man who can't stop the small ball. Think about that now over the weekend."

I did and by Monday morning I was even more determined.

"I want to take Yashin as my confirmation name, sir."

"I'll talk to your mother," he said.

In the end, it didn't come down to the small ball or Saints' names or any of that. It came down to my mother warning me that the Archbishop wouldn't confirm me, that the Holy Ghost wouldn't come down on me – or if he did it would only be to singe my sacrilegious soul, and probably my hair in a follow up air-strike –and that money doesn't grow on trees and my new short-trousers would be wasted and, worst of all, I'd have to sneak out the side door of the church in ignominy and the family wouldn't be able to show its collective face again till hell had frozen over.

And so I capitulated but not without tears and not without longing glances at my scrapbook pictures and not without a silent, sailing apology being whispered towards Russia – or where the sun rose in the mornings anyway.

And when I was asked what name I had chosen I said, "Paul" and then, under my breath, I muttered "Yashin."

But I bought the t-shirt and I still have it and I wear it sometimes in honour of Lev Yashin, the Black Spider, the greatest goalkeeper the world has ever known; the man who, ironically, lost his leg to cancer. But I wear it too in honour of the small boy who never really gave up on his hero.

Autumn

I'm no great lover of autumn. There's something about the mist, rather than the mellow fruitfulness, that throws long shadows with the earlier setting of the sun. And there's something about an impending birthday – and, yes, I know birthdays are always impending until impending becomes upending – something reminding me that time truly has speeded up and that the year seems hardly to have turned before it turns again.

I know there's much to love about this season. It lights the days with trees that go on fire as September steps between the windfalls into the arms of golden-haired October. There are days and weeks of nature's showy coats and dresses, breathtaking ribbons of reds and yellows, crimsons and bronze, but autumn will quickly shed each colour until all of them are gone.

And, yes, it does have other consolations. Branches curtseying to the wild, west wind, bent low with apples, their flesh sweetened by the gentle tap of frost; haw lanterns burning on the roadside; the final twirl and turn of climbing, fragrant woodbine in the ditches; dusky sloes that sharpen in the first clear, freezing night. The elderberries hanging low for picking. The last roses holding out against the end of time, their rich perfume – transplanted from house to house since 1958 – still catches me unawares outside the garden shed. And the clusters of damsons, packing the cluttered branches, shine like dark suns in the late morning light. The timber shed is full to the roof, last year's fallen trees sawn now and logged, piled neatly against the colder days of winter, their weathered ends creating satisfying patterns as I give the grass a final cut.

In the fields along the lane, the mushrooms elbow each other for space, pushing through the sun-warmed earth, littering the grass with button heads of white. All these are good things, each brings its own reward, but there's the deeper darkness that follows, that feeling that the year is sinking behind some kind of dusky horizon, disappearing from clear view, only to be seen from now through slanting rain and low clouds that will squat no more than fifty feet above the ground. Oh, yes, the sun will shine on the occasional winter day – a fleeting reminder of what's gone with the emigrant swallows.

In spite of all its transient beauties, there's something artificial about the season, a sense of the tentative and uncertain about these days. What autumn brings, in spite of its transitory beauty, is the imminence of endings and, yes, I fully realise that every season has that element of hesitation, of the proximity of something else, of something old and something new – of time inexorably passing. What autumn brings is a garish, burning brightness that is illusory. Autumn is the time spent in insecurity outside the headmaster's office. Winter is the outcome, for better or for worse and, often, the outcome is less frightening than that time of waiting outside the closed and doubtful door.

For now, I'll enjoy the fruits of these months but always in the full knowledge that tomorrow they will all be gone. Autumn will shed its leaves and drop its fruits into the winter earth, the shades will lengthen and the season will lose its temporary lustre. Yet, wonderfully, and only weeks from now, spring will begin to stir beneath the ground and the rising light creep closer day by blessed day.

Transit umbra, lux permanet.

Winter

Going for the Milk in November

The evening angelus was always the reminder my mother needed to send me *for the milk.*

Going for the milk wasn't about collecting a bottle or a carton from the shop. It was about taking the can from the back kitchen and heading for Mahon's farm, at the other end of Castledermot. In the summer time this was a dawdling journey, interrupted by stops for games of marbles, or a ten-minute halt to offer advice to younger boys fishing for pinkeens in the stream that ran by Carlow Gate. Occasionally, the milk can was called into service for these fishing expeditions. Being bigger and wider than jam-jars, there was a better chance of catching the small fish in it. They could then be transferred to the glass jars. Young as I was, I never told my mother about these occasional, if temporary, recyclings of the can. At ten years of age I might not know what discretion meant but I had some sense that it was, indeed, the better part of valour.

Going for the milk might also involve a detour into MacEvoy's or Savage's for sweets. One thing was guaranteed: spring, summer and autumn, the trip never took less than half an hour.

Once arrived at Mahon's, I'd wait for the can to be filled in the little dairy at the side of the house. If the cows hadn't been milked, I'd sit on the stone seat outside the dairy door, the collies licking my knees. But, more often than not, the milking was well over by the time I reached my destination and the milk was ladled, still tepid from a large churn, its warmth thawing the coldness of the metal can.

"Be sure the lid is tight now coming home," my mother would have warned.

"Be sure the lid is tight now going home," Mrs Mahon would echo.

And off I'd go on my equally circuitous return.

But that was spring, winter and autumn. Winter was another thing entirely.

By the time the angelus bell rang a thick darkness would have fallen on our village with its three street lights – none of which was close to Mahon's farm. The journey now involved walking down through Carlow Gate, across the School Lane, onto Church Lane and past the gates and wall of St James's church and graveyard. Alright to whistle past a graveyard in summer, but in the month of All Saints and All Souls it was a totally different experience.

There was another route to Mahon's, up by the Square and down Keenan's Lane but this involved passing the corner boys, permanent, shadowy fixtures beneath the streetlight on the village square and a Greek chorus to every child who passed. Seed, breed and generation would come under scrutiny; sisters and mothers were a subject for liberal comment. The two possible routes were a toss-up between fear of the living and terror of the dead. For some reason the dead always won.

So down I'd slink, from the darkness of Main Street to the deeper darkness of Church Lane, the gloomy forms of the church and the round tower rearing out of the pitch. But it was the trees that sheltered the greater terror. They leaned out over the wall, the wind whipping their branches together like the knitted clicking of skeletons and there were skeletons aplenty to rise and leer over the stones, their empty eyes and gritted teeth drifted out of the gloom, their bony elbows rested on the granite wall. I knew they were there. And I knew there were centuries of them lining up to watch me as I passed – hadn't I read the gravestones in the long and fearless summer days? Some dating back to 1617. So I'd tuck the can beneath my arm and run from my own clandestine hell with its ghosts and spirits, its floating spectres and its moaning bones, their wailing echoes in the trees above. I'd run and run until my little legs took me into the light of Mahon's yard – electric salvation leaking through their kitchen window and pouring its welcome from the open dairy door.

And Mrs Mahon would fill the can and say: "Be sure the lid is tight now going home."

"I will," I'd say. "I will."

And what I wanted to add, but never did, was that it would be as tight as tight could be because, once I got beyond the glowing yard, I'd need to brace myself for the race again, for the terror of the road that seemed even darker after the brightness of the dairy. I needed to hold the can and hold my nerve against the wailing souls whose every day – as far as I was concerned – was a preparation for these passings of mine. Their death-long ambition was to have me, to stretch across the wall and clutch my hair and face and spine with the bones that were the only fingers left to them, to drag me screaming wordlessly into an underworld of saints and souls.

There was only one possible escape. Check the lid again. Head down. And one, two, three ... now run for it, just run, run, run and keep on running for your life until you pass the open door of Doyle's and cross Main Street and – whatever else you do – just don't look back.

All Souls' Night

Maybe it's the process of getting older but I find myself having a shorter and shorter fuse when it comes to the things that irk me. It could be the four-wheel drivers who treat the morning school run as a way of boosting their flagging egos; it could be the rudeness of people in shops; it could be the way banks no longer want to deal with you face to face. But it's not. Today's gripe is with the spread of the phrase "he passed" or "she passed" when people speak of death.

For starters – death is not the Leaving Cert or a driving test. So why refer to people who have died as having *passed* or *passed over*. Has the sanitisation of life and death reached such a point that we can no longer refer to death by name? Are we foolish enough to believe that if we give something a new label we change what it's really about?

I'm not convinced that the past was a better place but there are things about it that really were less artificial and one of them was the way we dealt with death, after death had dealt with us.

Next Friday is All Souls' Day – the day on which we remember those who have dropped the L plates of Life and Living and moved on to another highway that's less cluttered...or so my *passing* friends would have me believe. My memory of childhood All Souls' Days – or more accurately All Souls' Nights – is much earthier; much closer to what the day is truly about.

My mother came from the West of Ireland and brought with her a basket of religious practices and beliefs and one of them was the tradition of visiting the graveyard on All Souls' Night. Come half seven or eight o'clock, the coats would go on, and she and I would troop through the village. My father would stay at home, reading the day's paper. He was never – to use his own words – into "that class of thing."

So my mother and myself would make our way through the village, across the School Lane and down Church Lane to St James' Church. I'm talking the early sixties here when the sole street light in Castledermot was on the Square. But, by the time we'd reached the gates of the graveyard, we'd grown accustomed to the darkness.

Stepping through the narrow stile was always a moment of uncertainty for me. The headstones – dating back to the seventeenth century; the Romanesque doorway; the high crosses and the round tower seemed, suddenly, to loom out of the murkiness like ogres. But my mother was having none of it.

"You brought your rosary beads?"

A quick fumble in my coat pocket.

"Yeah."

"Right, we'll start so."

And off we'd go, walking slowly round the graveyard path, reciting the sorrowful mysteries. The mantra of the repeated words and phrases had a calming effect on me. Mostly, I kept my eyes on the ground and my mind off the possibilities that might linger among the angled headstones. And then – inevitably – it happened. Year after year I prepared myself and year after year I was caught on the hop.

Rounding a corner of the church, or stepping past the dark curve of the tower, we'd stumble upon a figure moving slowly through the darkness, a low figure who seemed to emerge from the stonework or a lofty figure that stepped from the shape of a headstone and my skin would freeze, my blood run cold, my responses to the rosary would become a stutter until the figure spoke and I'd recognise the voice – the smaller figure, inevitably, was Mrs

O'Flaherty, the taller one Mrs McDonald. They seemed to be the only other people who did the rounds of the churchyard on All Souls' Night. And once the rosaries had been finished, my mother and her two companions would loiter in the shelter of the sycamores and chat, at ease with the dead about them, naming the names of friends who had died rather than *passed* in the previous twelve months.

Back then, I just wanted to get home, home to my comics or toy soldiers and to the warmth of the fire. But, viewed from this distance, it seems to me there was something essential and strangely vital about the practice of naming the dead and naming death for what it is. And I'm glad I was brought on the rounds of the graveyard on those dark and blustery nights. And I really do wish we could get rid of that awful and evasive phrase about *passing* and accept our own mortality in word as well as in deed.

All Souls' Day

Years and years, so many years ago.
We are driving west towards home
from somewhere near the coast,
that's all I now remember of the geography.
My father is almost a decade older than I am now.
I can't recall who's at the wheel –
it might be him; it might be me.
I do know spring is threatening,
but only in the deeper woods.
His wife, my mother, has been dead for just a month.
My heart keeps hammering, as though it's had six cups of coffee,
and with every cup I've tried to start this conversation.
It's like summoning a younger man's courage
to ask a girl to dance,
and, though the metaphor seems trite,
my question is about the dance of death,
doubly difficult since we've hardly spoken of my mother's recent death.
And now...and now...I want to know about the buried children,
their memory emerging in her ember days
though never in her lucid life.

We're on a long, true road when I find a voice and speak.
My father hesitates, then tells the *where* but not the *when*
and the stillborn numbers are vaguely unremembered.

I ask another question but he turns:

it's clearer now, I'm driving, he's the passenger.

'This is not something I want to talk about, what's said is said.'

The miles go past and we are almost home before he speaks again.

'If I could take my skin off,' is what he says, 'and start again,

I'd take off each mistake that goes with life.'

Are these words meant for him or are they meant for me?

Stephen

I have no idea where the time went, not the foggiest notion, but it's been fifty years since I first stepped into the Arts Block in Belfield, a rookie in this new world of third-level education. Coming from a school where the total student population was less than a hundred, this teeming building and teeming campus in a teeming city was a shock to me. All these people hurrying about their business and all of them, it seemed, knowing where they were bound and what they were doing and, worse still, all of them seeming to have lots of friends.

It took me a month or two to find my feet. Foolishly, perhaps, I spent the first couple of weekends in Dublin, wandering the city, hanging out at the Dandelion Market, waiting for the miracle of human connection to manifest itself. It didn't. At least not in those first few weeks.

But, little by little, I got to know people in my English and History and Philosophy classes. Faces gradually became familiar, names were exchanged and lunches were eaten in company rather than alone. I joined a couple of societies and, in one of these, I met the smiling Stephen Hilliard.

Stephen was five years older than me and he had a life and experience far beyond the confines of my sheltered secondary schooling. He'd worked as a street sweeper in London. He was an Irish-speaking member of the Church of Ireland. He was deeply interested in Christianity and socialism. He had a part-time job in *The Irish Times* as a sub-editor and sometime reporter on religious affairs. He had a speech impediment. He had a wonderful warmth about him. And, most importantly for those of us who knew him and were constantly penniless, he had a Morris Minor and was a generous chauffeur.

It's difficult, at this remove, to realise how great it was to have motorised transport in Dublin in the early seventies. I had a bicycle, donated to my college career by our neighbour, Mrs O'Connell. Otherwise, transport was by shank's mare or on the open backed platform of the 46A or the 10, always with an eye out for the bus conductor. A trip into the city centre from Belfield might involve three buses, with lightning quick exits – often while the bus was still moving – as the conductor went up or down the stairs in search of fares.

So, having Stephen as a friend not only opened a new world of debate and discussion and fun but it also provided regular transport to and from meetings and events in the city centre. With four or five or six of us crammed into the Morris Minor, the journeys were educational trips in the truest sense of that phrase.

Stephen was studying Irish, English and History and he never failed to provide copies of lecture notes to those of us who were otherwise engaged – in my case, playing endless World Cup matches on the back pitches in Belfield while lectures were proceeding without me in the Arts Block.

Stephen moved away from Belfield in 1973 while I remained there to do my H Dip in Education. Our paths crossed occasionally and I knew that he had gone on to study theology and, some years later, been ordained into the Church of Ireland. This was no great surprise. He had often spoken about his uncle, Bob Hilliard, who was not only a champion boxer and Church of Ireland Rector but who had gone to London, joined the Communist Party and volunteered to fight in the Spanish Civil War, dying in February 1937 as a result of wounds received at the Battle of Jarama. When he spoke about his uncle, it was clear where Stephen's Christian, socialist and radical roots lay.

And so, as often happens, a friendship that had blossomed in college became an occasional crossing of paths. I knew Stephen was working as a priest, somewhere in Dublin, and, from time to time, I'd meet someone who knew him and I'd send my best wishes.

And then, twenty-years after we'd met, and thirty years ago, I heard Stephen's name on a news report. He had just moved to Rathdrum in Co Wicklow, as Rector. There had been a break-in at the rectory and he had been killed.

Just recently, Stephen came again to mind, on the thirtieth anniversary of his death. Even now, it's hard to believe, to accept, that a man so filled with goodness and kindness and laughter could have been cut down so early in his life. When I remember him, I remember a laughing man, crouched over the steering wheel of the old Morris Minor, while we piled in behind him, ready for another trip, another lesson in life, another moment in a fleeting but wonderful friendship.

The End of the Season

"It's not the way it used to be. It used to be that soccer was the thing; the matches were what the game was about. Now it's just money, money, money. You look at the likes of Chelsea, that's a team that bought its way to the top."

I let the man ramble on. Where was the sense in interrupting him? He had a point about modern soccer being as much about money as it was about football. And I didn't tell him I'd been a Chelsea fan since 1963, a time when soccer was not about money and Chelsea finished an agonising second in the old first division, a point behind Stoke City. I didn't tell him that the only Chelsea shirt I own is the old plain blue one, made long before sponsorship became the multi-million-euro business it now is.

And nor did I tell him about my first visit to Stamford Bridge to watch Chelsea play. It was early November 1995 and my son, Ewan, then an eleven-year-old Chelsea supporter, and myself made the trip to London as a slightly belated birthday present to both of us.

The morning was passed in the club shop with all its gaudy knick-knacks and the afternoon was spent watching a less than inspiring 0-0 draw with Sheffield Wednesday. Afterwards, long after the stadium had drained its shouting throng into silence, we hung around outside the dressing room entrance, Ewan hoping against hope for some players' autographs. Eventually, the Sheffield Wednesday squad began to drift out in ones and twos and climb onto their team bus. But as for the Chelsea players – Kharine and Gullit and Sinclair and Hughes and Petrescu – not a sign was to be seen.

Keeping one eye on my watch and one on the entrance to the dressing rooms, I calculated – for the umpteenth time – just how long more we could hang on in hope and still catch our late evening flight.

The wind was blowing cold and darkness had long fallen and our only companion was the silent security man at the entrance. And then a door opened and the diminutive figure of Denis Wise appeared. Ewan stepped forward, autograph book in hand.

"You been waiting here all this time?" Wise asked, taking the pen and autograph book from Ewan. "Why didn't you come in?"

He glanced at the security man and smiled.

"You couldn't, could you?"

Ewan shook his head.

"Where are you from then?"

"Ireland."

"Terry Phelan is Irish."

He signed his name with a flourish and returned the autograph book.

"Tell you what," he said. "You just hang on there a mo," and with that he disappeared back inside.

The minutes passed, the darkness deepened and the night grew colder.

"We'll really have to get going in the next few minutes," I said, checking my watch again. "At least you got Denis Wise's autograph, that's something."

"But he told us to hang on," Ewan said quietly.

"I know, but we do have a plane to catch and we have to get across London. We'll give it five more minutes and then we really will have to leave."

As though he'd overheard our conversation, the dressing room door flew open and Denis Wise reappeared, a football tucked under his arm.

"I think I got all the lads to sign it," he said. "It's one of the match balls."

He placed the football in Ewan's hands. He might as well have been offering the Holy Grail.

"I hope we'll see you here again and hopefully, next time, we'll stick a few in the net."

And then he was gone.

Ewan carried that ball across London on the Tube; he carried it onto the plane and he carried it into the car at Dublin airport. It never left his hands and he slept with it beside his bed that night.

I didn't tell the story to the man who said the game is all about money because I didn't think he'd want to hear it. It wouldn't sit with his perception of the sport and the players. And I didn't tell him that ball still has pride of place in my son's old bedroom. I didn't tell him a lot of things. I just listened and nodded and knew that the truth is often otherwise and, after all the money has been paid and all the deals have been done, players are players and they have hearts and souls and are capable of kindnesses that often go unrecorded.

A Long Time Ago

It's a long time ago and I'm sitting in the kitchen of my friend's house on the Low Terrace. It's a cold wet evening with the wind lifting in from the east. The kitchen table is set for tea, crowded with mugs and plates and knives. There's a big pat of butter in the middle. One of the daughters of the house sits at the range, toasting bread on two long forks. As each side darkens, she turns the bread and toasts the other side. That done, she piles the slices on a huge plate that sits on top of the range and begins the routine again.

Suddenly the back door opens and the girl's father is blown in on the whistling gale. His coat is saturated with rain and his trousers are plastered against his legs. Shaking himself in the scullery, he kicks off his boots.

"Go in and put on your Sunday clothes," his wife says; "the supper is near ready."

My mother calls our evening meal tea but everyone else on the Low Terrace calls it supper.

The man passes through the kitchen, winking at me.

"Good man."

Five minutes later he's back, wearing the trousers of his Sunday suit, the only other clothes he owns. He carries his soaking work trousers, shirt and coat and hangs them on the sheila above the range. Immediately, steam begins to rise. He goes back into the scullery and I hear a tap running. When he returns, he's carrying his boots, stuffed with newspaper, and he puts them carefully between the legs of the range.

"Will we ate then?" he asks.

We gather round the table – the man, his wife, his children and me, the neighbours' child from up the road.

The woman sets a plate of steaming rashers, sausages, eggs, black and white pudding and fried potatoes before the man. The rest of the family ate dinner at midday. We sit and butter our toast and drink our tea.

"Well, how was school?" the man asks.

"It was good."

"It was all right."

"We got drenched coming home."

"Did yis not run between the drops? I used to run between the drops and I coming home from school?"

We laugh.

"Was this man's mother hard on yis?" he nods in my direction and smiles. "Did you know she was my first teacher?"

I shake my head.

"She was begor."

We finish our food and clear the table. I see my friend's father start to rise from his seat but then the energy goes out of him and he sits back down and lays his head on his folded arms and closes his eyes.

"Forty winks," he says quietly.

I notice the clay of the day's work still streaked high across his forehead. I see the cuts and gouges on the backs of his hands. I hear the depth of his breath as he draws it in and lets it out.

When I leave for home, an hour later, he's still asleep at the table, like one of the infants in school at rest time.

Two years have passed, home from boarding school for my summer holidays, I follow his coffin down the Low Terrace. He was a young man, still in his forties then, worn out by hard and bitter work.

The Gathering of Ghosts

It was a busy record shop with music blaring and an unrelated film playing on a large screen. There were staff members stocking shelves and customers coming and going, making the occasional enquiry about one artist or another. I was wandering pretty aimlessly, checking out the folk section before moving on to the other end of the shop and the stacks of vinyl that are, again, part and parcel of the music business. I leafed through the reissues of albums I'd bought in my teens and twenties and then, without warning, a sudden wave of sadness broke over me. And just as suddenly the shop seemed filled with the shadowy figures of young men and women I had known growing up and their younger brothers and sisters whom I had taught.

There were the shadows of students who had danced on Saturday nights, boys and girls who had jived and swayed in the almost derelict youth club in Castledermot in the early seventies; teenagers who had danced in the same decrepit building ten years later, when I worked in the village as a teacher. There was the smiling girl who was waked in her wedding dress a week before what should have been her wedding day; the young man whose life came to a sudden and untimely close on a moonlit road, the engine of his motorbike still roaring long after the life had gone from his broken body; the beautiful, laughing young woman whose life ended in childbirth. They and a dozen others jostled gently around me, looking over my shoulders, searching for a favourite album or song among the stacked racks of vinyl.

I listened carefully to their laughter and wordless chatter as they argued about the merits or otherwise of this band or that. I saw them frown over the names of singers who had surfaced long after they had gone, the frustration of unheard music and unlearned words furrowing their brows. What had they missed in leaving early, what tunes might they have whistled or sung had they lived longer?

And suddenly – on that cold, bright morning – a night fell. But what night? Any one of a hundred when the music played from the twin decks in the corner of that sad old building that was, for those three or four hours, transformed by coloured bulbs and the smell of weak coffee and the laughter of teenagers into everything that life had to offer – concern, nervousness, hope, love, a kiss, a word, a promise, an arrangement, the thought of a long, starlit walk home. And all the time the music played and the bodies swayed – slow or fast – and everything was possible.

My eyes fell on a couple dancing slowly, his arms wrapped protectively around her; her head on his shoulder. And they were lost in the shared dream of a life that lay ahead. And part of me wanted to tap them on the shoulders and tell them the truth that I knew about their lives but I didn't – couldn't. Instead, I let them dance away, enfolded by the music and possibility of the moment. Grief and loss would come in their own bad time. For now, I left them with their love and hope and wrestled with my own sadness, that emotion that comes trailing memory and the knowledge of what might have been.

I couldn't help but think of the lives that young couple had hoped for and aspired to but, for then, for that time between remembering and stepping back into the real world beyond the swinging doors of the record shop, I stood and watched them dance and listened to the Poppy Family singing, *Which Way You Going Billy?* and wished I could have warned them of the traps and snares that lay ahead.

But we live in the now and perhaps that is one of the saving graces of this life.

A Year Has Passed

Angela woke me in the early hours of that Friday morning with the news that our comrade was dead. And then the sun rose, as it always does, on to a cold and glorious morning. And that, too, seemed appropriate.

The first and second times I saw Leonard Cohen in concert were on an evening in the early seventies in the National Stadium in Dublin. I was a student but I'd managed to scrape together the money for a ticket to the first of his two shows that night. As I was hedging my bets and trying not to leave the Stadium, I met a fellow student, Luigi Rea, who was involved in the catering and he managed to get me back into the venue for the second show.

More than a decade would pass before I actually managed to meet Leonard. It was the mid-eighties and I was working as a producer in the then Radio 2. I'd gone, the morning after a Cohen concert, with the presenter Ken Stewart, to record a programme called "Favourite Five."

The recording done, I produced all my Cohen books and albums from a very large and tattered brown paper bag, asking uncertainly if he'd mind signing them. Not only did Leonard sign but each carried an individual message. Pushing my luck, I asked if there was a chance that I might get a photograph of him with my daughter, Lydia, who was in the corridor outside.

"Of course, of course," he said. "Bring her in."

And so the photograph was taken and we thanked him and prepared to leave.

"I'd like to give your daughter some candy," Leonard said. "I think there's some in my suitcase." At this, Lydia perked up, smiled and wriggled out of my arms. Standing right beside him, her eyes followed his every move as he unzipped the case and the search began but the elusive sweets could not be found.

"But you can't leave empty-handed," he added. "Why don't you have this?"

He unclasped a brooch from his jacket, a brooch in the shape of a guitar, and pinned it to my daughter's cardigan.

"I know it's not candy and I'm sorry I couldn't find some but I will...next time."

And that was the first gesture in a thirty-four-year friendship.

In the summer of 2016 a letter arrived to Lydia in the days before her wedding.

Dear Lydia and Brendan,
I am so happy to learn that you have found one another. May all the
blessings that life has to offer, may all these blessings be yours. With
love from your old friend, Leonard

Through the years Leonard was always there – the older, wiser brother moving on ahead, experiencing life and its losses and gains, sending back reports in his songs and poems and prayers.

And the letters went back and forth through those same years – at Christmas time; on the Jewish New Year; on birthdays:

dear bro
I warned you about this
but you keep getting older and older

One of the things I loved most about Leonard was his lack of pretence. He was an extraordinarily private person and yet he opened his heart and soul in his work. He was a genius, yet his humility was deep and real. This was the man who polished his own shoes before concerts; this was the mostly reclusive man who cooked and shopped for himself and shared a modest house on South Tremaine in Los Angeles. The humility and honesty that filled the songs were there in his life, in his beliefs and there, too, in his willingness to not hide, not pretend, not be the persona but always the person.

There were deeply dark times in Leonard's life. Years when CBS refused to release his work in the United States; years when his savings disappeared; the more darkly and deeply painful personal depressions. But always the work went on.

And always, always – in the songs, in the poems and in the letters – there was a glint in the eye and the sense of humour that those who dismissed his work as depressing seemed inexplicably to miss. For Leonard's eighty-second birthday I sent him a print of Frederic William Burton's wonderful painting, *Meeting on the Turret Stairs*. The reply came swift and humorous as ever:

thank you for the good wishes and the painting (like the rest of us, he doesn't know what he's getting into)
love
L

The sun rose up on that Friday morning with fire and passion, dear friend, with beauty and warmth, a reminder of all the gifts that were yours to us. By then you were buried in Montreal, buried without fuss or notice.

You left as you had lived, with style and grace and humility.
Sleep well, old friend, sleep well.

The Last Train

It's a wet Saturday afternoon. My father comes into the kitchen.

"We're going to Athy," he says.

"Can I stay here?"

I spend Monday to Friday at school in Athy. I don't want to spend a wet Saturday there as well.

"I'd like you to come. There's something I'd like you to see," he says.

"What?"

"Just something."

"I think you should come," my mother says.

I'm intrigued. This isn't like my parents at all. Normally they're only too happy for me to stay at home.

After we drop my mother at the Square in Athy, my father drives to the railway station. We get out of the Morris Minor, pulling on our raincoats, and walk up to the signal cabin, my father's workplace, where Joe Murphy is sitting at the fire, smoke drifting from the damp turf.

"Is she on?" my father asks.

"A couple of minutes," Joe says. "She's cleared Kildare."

I follow my father back down the slippery cabin steps, past the water tower and up onto the platform. We stand in the shelter of the waiting room and then we hear a train. My father steps out and I follow him. A black steam engine hoots beneath the town bridge, the arch damping the smoke and pushing it back into the open cab. Brakes scream out along the wet rails and the train comes to a halt. I follow my father down the platform. The engine driver leans over the side of the cab and greets us.

"A bad day for it," my father says.

"Rotten," the driver nods.

"Would you mind if we took a spin with you, out to Aughaboura Bridge?"

"Not at all. Hop up."

I'm lifted high in the air, up onto the metal running plate and I move between the driver and the stoker, in the hot, open cab. Rain spits off the boiler. My father climbs up after me. The signal changes and the huge engine grinds slowly down the line, past the signal box where Joe Murphy leans from the open window and salutes. The driver and stoker return his salute. On we go, past the siding, past the creamery, under Aughaboura Bridge. The brakes squeal again and the train grates heavily to a halt. My father climbs down and I follow him, carefully.

"Thanks," he says.

The driver and stoker wave as we step onto the wet grassy bank. The engine bucks, the flat wagons juddering and pushing against each other before the train picks up speed. The whistle sounds and the train disappears down the line to Maganey. My father watches it out of sight and then we turn and walk back along the track, the few hundred yards to the car.

"That's the last steam train through here," my father says. "I thought it'd be nice for you to be able to say you were on it."

We sit into the car and drive through the town, to meet my mother, and he never mentions that afternoon again.

For My Late Father on His 106th Birthday

Meeting my father at winter's end
in a half-walled garden,
stones stumbling to an emptied grave,
long grass fermenting
with apples dropped by wind and time,
picked almost to the seed by eager flocks.

Oh smell of other days,
of long life lost,
of rotting time.

All bitter rain has driven east,
new grasses grow
and we have met to celebrate.

I hope to meet him here again,
beneath the bursting branches
lit by silver blossoms and a yellow moon.

A Ghost in the Car

It's been thirteen years and I've never spoken or written about this. It's like a reason I can't find or an excuse I can't offer. Yet every time I pass the hospital I think of it and, just today, while I was driving, I heard a song called "Ghost in my Car" and I knew I had to write the story down because there is a ghost in my car and always will be, I suppose.

It was 1998 and the doctor had recommended – more than recommended, he had, to use his own words, "very seriously urged" – that my father should spend some time in the local hospital. It was a question of his need for medical care, the doctor said, a question of respite. It was, as we'd expected, a suggestion that my father resisted for a long, long time.

"It's for two weeks, just two weeks," I told him.

He nodded but was silent. The clock ticked. The fire burned.

"Two weeks has a way of becoming longer," he said at last.

"I know but, believe me, this is just for two weeks."

The matter was put aside, to be revisited whenever, and, of course, whenever might be never.

But my father's condition worsened.

"He really does need round the clock nursing at the moment," the doctor said. "It's not just advisable, it's imperative."

The subject was broached again, this time by the doctor. His mixture of charm and persistence, and a promise that my father would, definitely, be home in a few weeks, eventually swayed the argument and a date was set.

It was my responsibility to take my father to the hospital. Arriving at his house that lunchtime, I found him waiting,

"Available but not enthusiastic," as he said himself.

And so we set off, on the familiar ten-mile journey. The journey I estimated he had made twenty thousand times in a working life, twice a day; the journey that I had taken with him in my primary school years; the journey we had made winter and summer in the Morris Minor and, later, the Austin A40. Out past Mullaghcreelan Hill, down into Kilkea village; through Grangenolvin and Nicholastown and into Athy; over the railway bridge and past the railway station, where he had worked for most of his adult life. The great silence remained unbroken as we edged through the mid-afternoon traffic.

Over the Barrow bridge and right, onto the Stradbally Road, finally turning through the hospital gates, the imposing edifice, built in the Famine years, looming against the blue of the sky. Only then did my father speak. "I never thought you'd put me in the County Home."

To my father, this building would always be the County Home and the sight of its soaring, grey walls had brought almost ninety years of memory, suspicion and dread pouring out in that one sentence. To him, this was still the workhouse; the place where the unwanted, unrecognised, unkempt and undesired were dumped. It didn't matter that St Vincent's Hospital was and is a warm place, with an extraordinarily welcoming staff; it didn't matter that the facilities are modern; that he would be well nursed and well cared for or that he'd be coming home in a few weeks. He was a proud man and the stigma of the County Home, instilled in childhood, was still fresh, still raw, still humiliating.

He did come home that spring but the following autumn his doctor recommended another stint in the hospital. I didn't have the heart or soul – what am I saying? I didn't have the courage to drive him there on that occasion. Instead, I accepted my cousin, Peter's kind offer to be his chauffeur.

Scarlet Ribbons

(*for Dolores*)

It was a long time ago
and we three then, like the Magi,
are best viewed now from afar.
But as easy to unroll the passing time
as to furl a carpet back for dancing.

Your voice is sweet
and, better still, the way you sing
makes me believe in every word.
I never tire of the miracle,
those ribbons on the morning bed.

Not everything can be the way it was,
but hear the conversation fade
and the pin of rapt attention fall
on the silent New Year floor.

See the smiling faces in the glowing bells of light.
It's late
and someone calls for *one last song before we go*.
You sing that haunting tune.

Sing it.
Sing it again before we go.

Davy Ellard

When we moved to the new house, two years ago this month, it was a round-the-clock race to get each room painted before the floors went down. Late and early, we seemed to find ourselves on the tops of ladders or balanced on milk crates or straining from the edge of a chair to get that ... last .. bit ... just ... there ... in the corner. And then, finally, the house was painted and the floors were down and we began to consider the possibilities of not living out of boxes and not eating our meals from plates perched precariously on our knees. And after that, with the onset of the fine weather and the longer evenings, we considered the possibility of actually having the time to get out for a walk. And off we went, exploring the roads that had been so familiar to us on Google maps when the house search was on. And now here they were ... in the flesh ... or in the tarmac, wedged between the winding ditches and fields of County Carlow, fields that had begun to offer up their earliest blades of growth.

Not too far from home, on a bend in the road, we came across a cottage that was sparkling in the evening sun, its whitewashed walls glittering against the twilit sky; its garden immaculately kept and its patch of roadside verge bunched with flowers. And, across the road from the cottage, a seat had been built into the ditch, offering the ideal resting place for the weary walker, a spot from which to watch the sun go down behind the distant ridge.

Everything about the cottage and the garden spoke of years of loving care. We stopped a moment to take in the picture. From an orchard gate behind the house a Labrador barked a greeting and wagged his tail, but of the owner there was no sign.

We must have been on our third or fourth hike when, finally, we got to meet the proprietor of the gleaming house. He was in the garden sowing plants and we stopped to say hello and introduce ourselves. He said his name was Davy Ellard. He welcomed us to the area and wished us happiness and long life and, when we complimented him on his work, he smiled a diffident smile and shrugged.

"I used to have a lot more in the garden, vegetables and rhubarb and the like. I gave up growing rhubarb. I came home one evening and young fellows had got in and broken every stalk and pulled up every crown and thrown them round the road. I wouldn't mind if they'd taken them to eat."

A week later, my constant companion brought a home-made rhubarb tart to Davy's door.

Many mornings of last summer, I'd stop and chat with Davy and we'd compare notes on the state of our gardens and he'd fill me in on bits and pieces of local lore. And some mornings we'd discuss his health. He'd been in and out of hospital, he said, but he was hoping for the best. And his Labrador would come and stand by his side, occasionally raising a bark to suggest it was time I went about my business and let dog and man get on with theirs.

And then, as the last slow days drifted into the Indian summer that supplanted autumn, Davy was no longer in the garden. The hospital stays were longer now. Occasionally, I'd see a light in the house but I didn't call – you don't want to be disturbing people when they're just back home, I thought. And the garden went on sharing its colours and the dog went on barking his friendly bark and wagging his tail as I passed. And then, at last, the summer disappeared.

We buried Davy on the first day of this New Year, down in the cemetery at Wells.

Strange to pass his cottage on the way to his burial, still bright, still speaking of his pride; strange to see his dog behind the orchard gate, tail wagging as it always wagged but silent on that morning. And strange to be there in the burial ground that he and other local people had maintained so well across the years.

What we only learned on that raw morning, as we gathered in the cemetery, was that Davy had for years been the gravedigger in Wells. It was something he had never brought up in all our chats across his garden wall. Maybe he thought it wasn't the kind of thing you mention in polite conversation.

Coming new to an area, there are some things you learn by observation and some you learn with time. And there are people whose warmth and welcome put you at your ease, to such an extent that you feel like you've known them all your life. But some things you learn only through experience, like watching the other gravediggers shovel the dark clay onto Davy Ellard's grave.

The Three Wise Men

They came, each Christmas of my childhood, the three wise men.

The first was Andy Kelly. He lived three doors down from us in Abbeylands and he appeared – not by choice, on his part, but out of necessity on ours, every Christmas Eve afternoon. My mother had a tradition of not putting the Christmas tree up until Christmas Eve and, though the spirit was willing to get it in place on the morning of that day, the fact that was there was so much else to do in the house that it was always mid- to late afternoon before I was sent to bring it in from its resting place in the garage.

There were no such things as Christmas-tree holders back then – at least not in our house. Instead, an enamel bucket did the trick. Timber logs, stones and the odd briquette were lodged about the base of the tree to keep it steady and, once the tree was straight, the bucket was covered in red crepe paper. Then the decorations and lights were retrieved from the attic and the tree was bedecked. Finally, the lights were plugged in and that's where Andy Kelly, the first of the wise men, made his appearance. The lights never worked at the first time of asking or, if they did, they blew a fuse on the board in the hall, plunging the house into mid-winter darkness – a darkness that always seemed to take my mother by surprise!

"Run down and ask Andy Kelly if he'd mind having a look at them," my mother would tell me and I'd traipse along the terrace, wondering why I always got the job and speculating on the ill-timed magic that ensured that the lights went from working perfectly on 7 January of any year to not working on 24 December of the same year, when they had spent the intervening period resting in a box in the attic. Was there some malevolent sprite up in the dark roof space, so bored that he spent the summer and autumn months unscrewing bulbs and loosening wires?

And so I'd knock on Kelly's door and explain the situation and Mrs Kelly would tell me that her husband would be "down in a minute" and, sure enough, Andy would arrive in no time, find the fault and mend the fuse with a piece of silver paper from a cigarette packet – "just for the time being" – and promise to "have a look at the fuse-board once we get over the Christmas."

His electrical wisdom was a mystery to me – to all of us – but it never failed and never left us in the dark.

The second wise man was my brother, Jarlath. In his days as an arts student and then as a medical student in UCD, he worked as a temporary seasonal sorter and postman in Dublin. This meant that he never got home until late on Christmas Eve, coming on the last train to Athy, where my father would collect him. By the time they got to our house, my mother, my sister, Dolores, and myself would have all the stuffing and cooking and floor-washing and polishing done; the fires would be blazing in the kitchen and sitting room and the crib would be up, the candle lit in the window and the Christmas tree twinkling. The first sight of my brother coming through the back doorway always lifted my spirits to a new place and made Christmas real at last. The days of rest and joy and laughter had truly begun.

He would sit with us at midnight Mass; he would laugh with his friends in the churchyard afterwards; he would regale us with stories of life in Dublin, and one year he arrived with a record player he'd bought and three LPs – borrowed from Frank McDonald, the village butcher.

When my brother arrived home on Christmas Eve, the possibilities widened; the laughter deepened; the wonder of the season grew even more breath-taking. I think it had to do with the fact that he was ten years older than me and that I had total faith in his ability to solve all and any problem that came our way. He knew things, he solved things, he shouldered things – he was a wise and funny man.

The third wise man was one I never met, though once I heard the jangling of his sleigh-bells and the thump of his sleigh as it landed on the roof. He came in the small hours and his wisdom was matched only by his generosity. He knew what I had asked for and he saw to it that it was delivered, with a little more besides. And always there were books – unasked for but a source of wonder, pleasure and inspiration.

Two of these three wise men sleep now in cemeteries near Castledermot, their wisdom evoked, their hearts still warm in the place we treasure as memory. And the third? The third still comes in the dead of night – his wisdom undiminished.

John MacKenna

The Christmas Thief

Writers are thieves. We steal stories, ideas, phrases, characters, whatever we can lay our hands on and we do it at the drop of a hat. And we steal all the time – even at Christmas.

What I'm about to tell you is really the story of five men – the thief, his two friends, the man who lived on the roadside and the man in the London flat.

It was across a Christmas table that I first heard the story of the old man who lived on the roadside and it came from my neighbour, Paul Donohue. He mentioned that the old man had lived in a caravan on the outskirts of a nearby town. The caravan had been the old man's home for a long, long time. So long that he had cut back the ditch around it, dug and sown a vegetable patch, cleared and planted flowerbeds and made a lawn. The caravan and its garden were as well kept as any of the manicured gardens in the nearby estates. The man who lived on the roadside left people alone, went his own way and lived his patient, quiet life and, for the most part, people allowed him his peace.

On a particularly bright and calm Christmas morning a neighbour was making his way to Mass and, as he approached the caravan, he heard a low, whirring sound. Drawing closer, he saw the old man steadily walking up and down, pushing an outdated manual lawnmower, cutting the small patch of grass that bordered the vegetable garden. The men exchanged greetings and talked about the mildness of the day.

"It's unusual to see someone out cutting the grass on a Christmas morning," the neighbour said.

The old man looked him in the eye.

"Is it Christmas Day?" he asked. "I didn't know it was Christmas Day."

The second story was told to me by my friend Tom Hunt. And, again, it was told across a kitchen table at Christmastime. It was the story of Tom's father and uncle, who had worked on their father's farm. On his death, the farm was left to Tom's father, the eldest son. He assured his brother that he was welcome to stay on the land, that they could work side by side, but the younger man wouldn't hear of it and took the boat to England. Like so many before him, he found employment on building sites. And each Christmas Tom's mother would send a card to her brother-in-law, wishing him peace and the joys of the season.

"Thirty-eight years after he left home, the word came that he had died," Tom told me. "I was sent over to London to make the funeral arrangements and to clear out his flat. It was a single bedsit with one narrow bed, one chair, one table, one of everything. And under the bed I found the old cardboard suitcase he'd brought with him when he left home as a young man. And inside it were the thirty-eight Christmas cards my mother had sent him over the years. Nothing else. Just the Christmas cards."

I am a thief but sometimes a tale is too precious to steal.

I listened to the stories told me by Paul and Tom – over the same Christmas table as it happens – and I knew I could never do anything with them beyond retelling the isolation of the lives of the old man on the roadside and the man in the tiny London bedsit. Sometimes that's all there is to do. Sometimes you sit back and let the shiver of sadness run down your spine, the recognition of the roads and boats you might have taken. Sometimes you breathe in the blessings that are yours, gratefully accepting the happier share.

So tonight I think of the thief and his two friends sitting at a well-laden table in a warm kitchen, the lights from the Christmas tree falling across their faces. And I think, too, of the old men in their isolation and the strange appropriateness of their stories at Christmastime. For, are we not celebrating the birth of a baby boy whose existence was one of wandering and of homelessness and whose life ended in the most abject and isolated of circumstances?

But, if we believe what we're told, there was more to his story than that and my wish is that when Paul and myself sit across a Christmas table, in the glow of this year's seasonal lights, we will raise a silent salute to the memory of the old man in the roadside caravan; the man in the small London flat and to our absent friend, Tom Hunt, and wish them a happy and peaceful Christmas together in the brighter lights of eternity.

Stephen's Day

Stephen's Day – it was never St Stephen's day – that day when I could have been out on *the Wran* but wasn't; that day when I should have gone with my friends to the matinee but didn't; that day when I might have had a lie-in but couldn't. And all for the same good reason; the trip to Tuam, the annual pilgrimage from east to west; out of the sleeping village that was home; across the midlands in the Morris Minor – ZW2486 – from the back seat of which we'd glimpse *wran* boys and girls going about their own pilgrimage, house to house and door to door, gathering the goodies that they, no doubt, would share at the matinee in their local cinemas. Oh, how I envied them.

On through dozing towns and villages, the streets still Christmas quiet, the curtains undrawn; the cats curled up like tea cosies on windows, waiting for the first signs of life; the milk bottles nesting on doorsteps; not a trickle of smoke from any chimney – and why would there be? It was still early morning.

We stop off in Moate and sit in the cousins' kitchen, our parents drinking tea while I keep an eye on the half-open box of Black Magic on the edge of the table, waiting for my aunt to make the offer I can't refuse. Then I stuff as many sweets into my mouth as possible – while my older brother and sister frown on my bad manners. But it's worse than that. By the time we cross the bridge in Athlone I can feel the sweets regurgitating; they move and stick and rumble and shift like an avalanche in my throat.

"Hang on," my father says. "Hang on till I find a gate."

Then a quick exit and I reacquaint myself with the sweets. They come up whole.

225

"You didn't even chew them," my mother says.

"Disgusting," my sister adds as I climb back in. I get a window seat this time – just in case.

A couple of miles down the road, my brother starts to sing quietly.

That old black magic has me in its spell.

that old black magic that you weave so well,

those icy fingers up and down my spine....

"Enough!" my mother says and my brother falls silent, still smiling. The towns and villages pass. And the rain begins to fall.

Tuam is as Tuam always seems to be – wet, beneath a sky drenched with the smell of turf-smoke.

My grandmother has the table set and we sit in to a second Christmas dinner in two days. My mother warns me not to rush my food, my brother grins again. After the meal is over, the cousins and aunts and uncles descend and I find myself walking through the empty streets with the younger cousins, down to the only sweet shop that opens on Stephen's Day. We spend the money we've been given, then meander back to our grandparents' house in Church View.

In the window the Christmas candle is lighting and, inside, the table is being readied for tea. This will be followed at half-nine or ten o'clock by "a cuppa before ye go."

Then it's back into the Morris Minor. The seats are cold, the car is cold, the heater runs on candle power, it seems to me, but before we're well clear of the town my mother starts the rosary. By the time she reaches the third Glorious mystery, I'm fast asleep. I come to now and then and mumble: "Where are we?" and the word comes back from the front seat – Loughrea or Tullamore or Geashill and I drop off again, dreaming of the *Wran* and the cinema and the matinee I've missed.

Then suddenly I'm awake. The car has stopped and my brother lifts me onto his knee while my sister makes room on the narrow back seat. I hear running feet. Outside the night is pitch. The door opens and I see the faces of two girls from Castledermot.

"Thanks very much," one of them says.

They scramble in. I can smell their perfume.

"We thought we'd have to walk all the way home," the second girl says as the overloaded car pulls slowly away.

"Were ye in Dreamland?" my mother asks, naming the dancehall in Athy.

"We were."

"And was it good?" my father wants to know.

"The band was good. But that was it." The first girl giggles and her soft voice and her laughter are an anaesthetic to me. And, when I wake again, it's morning and I'm in my own bed and Stephen's Day is over and the pilgrimage has been made – for another year.

A New Year Gift

So here we are, creeping through the first uncertain days of a new year, leaving behind the remnants of the ancient. If the last days of the old year are about looking forward, perhaps the early days of the new year are for looking back and, when I cast my mind over the turnings of other Decembers, there are a couple that shine like Christmas candles.

One was a New Year's Eve in the early two-thousands. We spent it on Inis Mór and the weather, not surprisingly, was wild and wet and blustery. Nevertheless, we tramped the afternoon roads that wound between fuchsia bushes, stripped bare of their summer bells. We scrambled over stone walls and crossed a field to visit Assurnaidh's church and, as darkness began to fall, made our way, tired and windblown, back to the house. The meal that followed went on over several hours, the laughter growing warmer, the reminiscences rising like slow rivers and the stories ebbing and flowing across the welcoming table.

And then, just before nine, the phone rang and word came of a plane in trouble a hundred miles out, over the wilful waters of the bleak Atlantic, a plane flying from Newfoundland to Germany, a four-seater with just the pilot on board, a plane that was leaking fuel and needed to land at the first available airfield. And that was Inis Mór. The only problem was the lack of lights on the runway and so, as often happens in small communities, phones started ringing and the word went out that cars were needed to provide the lights that would illuminate the landing strip for the troubled aircraft and its pilot.

I had never experienced anything like this and neither had my ten-year-old stepson, Eoin, so we crowded into the car and travelled to the airfield, just a mile southeast of Kilronan. By the time we arrived other cars were edging through the gate and following directions to form lines along the sides of the runway. The dipped headlights would guide the pilot safely down.

Once parked, we stepped out and stood at a safe distance from the cars.

"Has this happened before?" I asked.

"It has," I was told. "The winter before last we got the same call and we came down to light the runway and we waited. But that plane was lost, out there, off the coast. And the pilot was lost. With the help of God tonight's flyer will have better luck."

I glanced at Eoin and, in the reflected half-light, noticed that he was carrying something.

"What's that?"

"A box of Heroes chocolates," he said quietly. "I brought them to give to the pilot when he lands."

We stood in the cold night air and watched the empty darkness that was the western sky. I strained to hear above the wind, imagining the sound of a small plane in the gloom. I pictured the pilot in the confines of the tiny cockpit, his fuel gauge slithering towards empty, his eyes straining for some sign of a light that might promise salvation. And I saw him peering through the darkness beneath his little plane, his face lit by the dim glow of the control panel, his only companion the ghost-reflection in the window at his side. And I glanced again at Eoin, clutching his box of chocolates, waiting for this man, this heroic figure, to land his damaged plane by the lights of the cars and to step onto the welcoming tarmacadam of the airfield. I saw a child waiting to offer this small yet wonderful reward to a man who had survived in spite of everything.

And then the word came. We could all go home. We need not spend the midnight that bridges one year into another on the windswept airstrip. The plane would not be landing here. The pilot had made it safely to Shannon.

"Buíochas le Día," a woman said.

I looked at the unopened box of chocolates in Eoin's hand and I wished the unknown airman a peaceful night and a restful sleep. And I wished him, too, some intimation of a young boy's big-hearted and gracious New Year's gift.

John MacKenna is the author of twenty-one books - fiction; memoir; biography; children's books and poetry.

He is a winner of the Hennessy; Irish Times and Cecil Day Lewis literary awards, and of a Jacobs Radio Award for his documentary series with Leonard Cohen. He is also the author of a dozen stage productions and a number of radio plays. His play *Lucinda Sly*, produced by RTE Radio 1, was a winner of the silver medal at the Worldplay Festival in New York. He teaches creative writing at Maynooth University.

Acknowledgements

Sincere gratitude to Jonathan Williams; Katie Jacques; Angela Keogh; Dolores MacKenna; Mark Turner; Sinead Dowling, Kelly Mooney and Aileen Nolan at Carlow Co Co Arts Office.

Thank you to David Mallett for his kind permission to reprint the lyrics of his wonderful song, from which I stole/borrowed the title of this book.

Thanks to Artl!nks for support in the preparation of this work.

And a particular thank you to Sarah Binchy, Clíodhna Ní Anluain, Aoife Nic Cormaic and Carolyn Dempsey at Sunday Miscellany, where these essays first appeared.